The Creative Entrepreneur

Unlocking Opportunities for Venture Success

The Creative Entrepreneur

Unlocking Opportunities for Venture Success

FALIH M. ALSAATY

Copyright © 2025 by Falih M. Alsaaty

All rights reserved. No part of this publication may be reproduced, distributed, or transmitted in any form or by any means, including photocopying, recording, or other electronic or mechanical methods, without the prior written permission of the copyright owner and the publisher, except in the case of brief quotations embodied in critical reviews and certain other noncommercial uses permitted by copyright law. For permission requests, write to the publisher, addressed "Attention: Permissions Coordinator," at the address below.

ARPress
45 Dan Road Suite 5
Canton MA 02021
Hotline: 1(888) 821-0229
Fax: 1(508) 545-7580

Ordering Information:
Quantity sales. Special discounts are available on quantity purchases by corporations, associations, and others. For details, contact the publisher at the address above.

Printed in the United States of America.

ISBN-13:   Paperback   979-8-89676-242-3

Library of Congress Control Number: 2025901204

Table of Contents

Preface I
Dedication III
About the Author. V

Chapter 1
Navigating the Path to Entrepreneurial Success

Chapter Objectives 1
What Constitutes Entrepreneurship? 2
Who is an Entrepreneur? 3
What Do Entrepreneurs Do? .3
What Skills Should Entrepreneurs Have? 4
The Role of Principles in Entrepreneurship 4
How to Choose Your First Business Venture
as a New Entrepreneur? 9
Summary 10
Questions 11
Appendix 1 12

Chapter 2
Innovation: The Magical Engine

Chapter Objectives 17
The Need for Self-innovation and Creativity 18
What's Innovation? What's Invention? 18
Types of Innovation. 19

Innovative Leaders: The Entrepreneurs 21
Country Ranking in Entrepreneurship 21
The Role of Innovative Entrepreneurs. 22
The Innovation Ecosystem 23
Creativity. 23
Attributes of Creative Individuals. 24
Creative Individuals Across Various Fields 25
Summary. 25
Questions. 26
Appendix 2 27

Chapter 3
The Innovative Mindset

Chapter Objectives 30
The Human Mind 31
What's a Mindset? 32
The Two Types of Mindsets. 33
Research Findings: The Impact of Mindset 35
Developing a Growth Mindset 37
Summary. 38
Questions. 39
Appendix 3 40

Chapter 4
Self-Innovation

Chapter Objectives 45
What's Self-innovation? 46
The Genesis of Self-innovation 48
Self-Determination Theory (SDT) 48
Social Cognitive Theory (SCT) 49

Self-Efficacy Theory (SET) .50
Diffusion of Innovation Theory (DIT) 50
The Psychology of Entrepreneurship 51
Summary. 52
Questions. 53

Chapter 5
Cultivating Personal Growth for Entrepreneurial Success

Chapter Objectives. 55
What's Personal Growth?. .56
Benefits of Personal Growth 56
Planning for Self-growth 57
Entrepreneurial Essential Competencies 58
Theories on Creativity and Innovation 59
Summary. 60
Questions. 61
Appendix 4 62

Chapter 6
Insights into Creativity Theories

Chapter Objectives. 66
Assessing Creativity. 67
The Componential Theory of Creativity 68
Sternberg's Investment Theory of Creativity 69
The Social Network Theory of Creativity. 70
The Four C Model of Creativity 70
The Four Ps of Creativity 71
Summary. 72
Questions. 73
Appendix 5 75

Chapter 7
Design Thinking for Creativity and Innovation

Chapter Objectives 79
Skills Categories 80
What's Design Thinking? .83
Design Thinking: The stages 83
Design Thinking vs. Traditional Problem-Solving Approach . . .84
Design Thinking and Entrepreneurship. 85
Summary 86
Questions. 87

Chapter 8
Design Thinking Techniques

Chapter Objectives 88
Empathizing 89
Persona Creation 92
The Six Thinking Hats 95
Summary 98
Questions. 99

Chapter 9
Positive Reinforcement and Entrepreneurial Success Factors

Chapter Objectives 100
Positive Reinforcement 101
Examples of Positive Reinforcement in Organizations: 102
Entrepreneurial Success Factors 103
The Road to Success 105
Summary 105
Questions. 106

Chapter 10
Artificial Intelligence (AI): The Entrepreneur's Weapon

Chapter Objectives 109
AI and Entrepreneurs. 109
What's AI? 110
What is AI Technology?. 110
Deployment of AI Technology 113
Benefits of AI Deployment 114
Summary. 115
Questions. 116

Chapter 11
Managing Your Own Company

Chapter Objectives. 118
What is Management? 119
What are the Managerial Functions? 119
Management Principles. 120
Company Structure and Strategy 121
Challenges Facing New Entrepreneurial Companies 123
Company Performance. 123
A Theoretical Framework for Management 124
Summary. 126
Questions. 127
References 128

Preface

The Creative Entrepreneur: Unlocking Opportunities for Venture Success is an important guide for anyone seeking to merge creativity with business acumen. Traditional business thinking often proves inadequate in addressing the rapidly evolving global competitive environment and technological advancements. This book highlights the importance of innovative thought and adaptability, providing readers with the tools to identify and seize new business opportunities. It empowers individuals to transform their passions into profitable ventures, achieving financial independence and influence. Furthermore, the book emphasizes the role of a creative mindset in cultivating business resilience. It offers practical advice on navigating the complexities of the modern entrepreneurial landscape.

This concise yet comprehensive book is designed to meet the needs of aspiring entrepreneurs looking to enhance their mindset, skills, and understanding of business opportunities, particularly within the U.S. economy. Compact and convenient, it offers wealth of practical information in a clear, accessible style free from technical jargon. Within these pages, you'll find essential topics relevant to today's dynamic business practices and economic landscape. Key areas of focus include:

- **Innovation and Self-Innovation**: Discover the secrets to entrepreneurial success by exploring the crucial role of innovation in both personal and professional life. Learn how a forward-thinking approach can help you excel in a competitive marketplace.

- **Creativity**: Dive into the world of creativity and learn how to harness its power to develop original solutions, revitalize existing concepts, and bring your entrepreneurial vision to life.

- **Personal Growth and Motivation**: Cultivate successful entrepreneurs' essential qualities and habits through personal growth strategies. You will build a strong foundation for your entrepreneurial journey by prioritizing self-improvement.

- **Design Thinking and Associated Techniques**: Gain valuable insights into the design thinking process and its practical applications for solving complex problems, fostering empathy, and driving innovation.

Dedication

This book is dedicated to the inspired, resilient, and courageous generation of entrepreneurs who will propel technological advancement and foster economic prosperity for our nation and, hopefully, the rest of the world, too.

About the Author

Dr. Alsaaty is a Professor of Management in the Management, Marketing, and Public Administration Department at the College of Business, Bowie State University, Maryland. He received his MBA and PhD degrees from the Graduate School of Business Administration (Stern School of Business), New York University, New York. Dr. Alsaaty has extensive teaching and research experience in Management, Business Strategy, and Entrepreneurship. He taught at several universities in the United States and abroad. Dr. Alsaaty has numerous publications in professional journals. In addition, he has authored and co-authored the following books in recent years:

- Driving Digital Transformation - Business Strategies for Entrepreneurial Success (2024).
- Entrepreneurial Edge - Essential Skills for Business Success (2023).
- Entrepreneurial Reach (2012).
- Launching and Managing New Ventures (2007).

Chapter 1
NAVIGATING THE PATH TO ENTREPRENEURIAL SUCCESS

> "An entrepreneur is someone who has a vision to something and a want to create."
>
> David Karp

Chapter Objectives

- To enhance understanding of entrepreneurship.
- To learn how to become a visionary entrepreneur.
- To grasp the essential steps of entrepreneurial success.
- To evaluate one's tendency for an entrepreneurial journey.

In recent years, a wave of entrepreneurs has swept across the United States and the globe. These creative minds have built remarkable companies in diverse industries, from social media and education to computers, software, airlines, travel, and many more. Many successful companies we know today, both domestically and internationally, owe their existence to visionary entrepreneurs. Microsoft, Dell, Nvidia, Amazon.com, Tesla, Toyota, Mercedes-Benz, and Nestle are all testaments to this. These companies have significantly contributed to national and international progress by creating jobs and delivering innovative products and services.

Entrepreneurial ventures are, in fact, a major driver of innovation and economic growth. The link between entrepreneurship, innovation, and economic prosperity is not only real but deeply rooted, and it is a topic widely discussed in both business and academic circles. This chapter delves into the core principles that guide entrepreneurs, explore their business visions, and examine the personality traits that define entrepreneurial thinking.

What Constitutes Entrepreneurship?

Many curious individuals wonder about the nature of entrepreneurship: Is it a career, an activity, or a field of study leading to a degree? The answer is yes; it can be all of these. In this book, however, we focus on entrepreneurship as a career path and a process. It aims to identify and capitalize on untapped economic opportunities through strategic thinking and resource allocation[1].

This definition implies the following:

- Entrepreneurs seek to discover or create new business opportunities, leading to new industries and economic sectors.

- Opportunity creation can be driven by profit motives (commercial entrepreneurship) or social goals (social entrepreneurship).

- Entrepreneurs employ strategic thinking to identify or create these opportunities.

- Entrepreneurs develop an attainable vision for their ventures to serve as a long-term guide for their sustainable growth.

- Entrepreneurs leverage resources such as people, technology, and facilities to establish ventures that produce goods and/or services.

- Successful entrepreneurs deliver innovative, desirable, and in-demand products or services.

---

[1] Entrepreneurship is also defined as "a discipline that seeks to understand how opportunities are discovered, created, and exploited by whom, and with what consequences." Neck, Heidi M. et al. (2018). *Entrepreneurship*, Thousand Oaks: California, Sage Publications, Inc. p. 6.

Who is an Entrepreneur?

An entrepreneur is a venture creator, investor, and individual whose business aspirations differ from typical, ordinary individuals[2]. Entrepreneurs are meticulous in venture creation, management, and growth. No correlation should be assumed between a venture's success and the entrepreneur's college education, nationality, ethnicity, gender, or geographic location. The venture's success is influenced by numerous factors, including:

- The entrepreneur's vision, strategies, leadership, and product/market knowledge.
- The venture's talent, funding, technology, and network resources.
- The quality, convenience, and price of goods/services offered.
- The nature of goods/services offered and whether they are essential to consumers or luxury products.
- The intensity of market competition.
- The state of the economy reflects consumer demand for goods and services.
- Government attitudes toward entrepreneurial companies as reflected in laws and regulations.
- Other external factors, such as natural disasters.

What Do Entrepreneurs Do?

Entrepreneurs typically progress through various stages in their careers. This journey starts with a would-be entrepreneur with an idea and then progresses to a nascent (or fledgling) entrepreneur who launches their first venture. Experienced entrepreneurs who build several successful companies become serial entrepreneurs. Finally, some achieved

---

[2] An entrepreneur is also viewed as the "one who creates a new business in the face of risk and uncertainty for the purpose of achieving profit and growth by identifying significant opportunities and assembling the necessary resources to capitalize on them". Scarborough, Norman M. and Cornwall, Jeffrey R. (2019). *Essentials of Entrepreneurship and Small Business Management*, Pearson Education, Inc.

international recognition, like Elon Musk (Tesla), Jeff Bezos (Amazon.com), and Warren Buffett (Berkshire Hathaway).

The intensity and rigor of an entrepreneur's tasks, functions, and responsibilities vary throughout their career. However, all entrepreneurs engage in the following activities, albeit at varying levels and with different roles:

- Leadership: Businesses require leadership to guide the team and achieve goals.

- Strategic planning and decision-making: Entrepreneurs make strategic choices regarding innovation, funding, resource allocation, and recruitment.

- External relations: Building and maintaining relationships with customers, suppliers, and relevant organizations is crucial.

- Internal communication: Effective communication with managers, supervisors, employees, and shareholders is essential.

What Skills Should Entrepreneurs Have?

Due to their leadership and decision-making positions, an entrepreneurial career demands a wide range of soft (human) and hard (technical) skills. Business education, including essential accounting, finance, management, and marketing knowledge, is crucial for business success. These areas of knowledge enable the entrepreneur to understand organizational functions, finance, strategies, operations, management, and markets. Some authors[3] list approximately thirty skills required for entrepreneurship, including oral communication, interpersonal skills, network building, decision-making, goal-setting, negotiation, persistence, risk-taking, and innovation.

The Role of Principles in Entrepreneurship

Entrepreneurship principles provide a guiding framework for leadership, innovation, strategic planning, and business practices. They constitute

---

[3] See, for example, Hisrich, Robert D. and Peters, Michael P. (2002). *Entrepreneurship*, Boston: Massachusetts, McGraw-Hill/Irwin, Inc.

the overarching structure within which ventures are conceived, managed, and cultivated. For aspiring, successful, and creative entrepreneurs, mastering fundamental entrepreneurship principles is crucial to avoiding failure and maintaining a competitive edge.

These principles encompass various aspects of entrepreneurial endeavors. Understanding and applying these principles is essential for entrepreneurs to establish and maintain sustainable businesses. Each principle often intersects with others, forming a comprehensive system that supports entrepreneurial success. By grasping these foundational elements, entrepreneurs can create robust foundations for their ventures, fostering growth and resilience in an ever-evolving, high-tech, and artificial intelligence-oriented business landscape. Key entrepreneurship principles are discussed below:

Visionary Thinking

Visionary entrepreneurs differ from many small business owners in several key ways. Unlike mom-and-pop establishments, visionary entrepreneurs are long-term thinkers with a clear vision for their venture and its desired destination. They possess persistence and determination, qualities that successful entrepreneurs such as Elon Musk (Tesla) and Jeff Bezos (Amazon) exemplify. Visionary entrepreneurs demonstrate exceptional foresight in identifying and transforming unseen market opportunities into new lucrative businesses and thriving industries. They exhibit creativity[4] and innovation[5] in decision-making and business dealings.

Innovative Approaches to Problem-Solving

A visionary entrepreneur is a creative, forward-thinking individual who delves deeply into a business enterprise's strategic issues, such as adapting to new technologies or expanding globally. These and other challenges require thoroughly analyzing upcoming decisions' benefits and drawbacks. A visionary entrepreneur is a skilled risk assessor,

---

[4] According to the American Psychological Association, creativity is "the ability to produce or develop original work, theories, techniques, or thoughts. A creative individual typically displays originality, imagination, and expressiveness." dictionary.apa.org.
[5] Merriam-Webster dictionary defines creativity as "a new idea, method, or device." or "the introduction of something new." www.merriam-webster.com.

efficiency optimizer, and opportunity seeker. They lead the enterprise with a clear vision, inspiring others with innovative ideas and firm conviction. Examples of visionary entrepreneurs include Bill Gates and Paul Allen (founders of Microsoft), Larry Page and Sergey Brin (founders of Google), Jack Ma (founder of the Chinese Alibaba Group), Masayoshi Son (founder of the Japanese SoftBank Group), and Carlos Slim Helú (founder of the Mexican Grupo Carso).

Calculated Risk-Taking

A calculated risk-taker is an individual with an analytical mind who focuses on evaluating decision outcomes for risks and rewards without avoiding excessive risk, especially in major business decisions. Visionary entrepreneurs tend more often than not to take calculated risks in organizational settings such as financial, recruitment, marketing, logistics, and other main business functions. These individuals consider facts and figures and conduct cost-benefit analyses. They do not assume important obligations without thorough thinking and consultation.

For example, in pursuing business strategies such as integration (forward integration, backward integration, horizontal integration), visionary entrepreneurs and their teams would analyze all aspects of the strategy, including its long-term effects on the company's financial health, growth prospects, and competitive advantage.

Talent Acquisition Strategies

Entrepreneurial companies in the early stage of their development typically exhibit several key characteristics:

- Small size and limited market experience.
- Recent origin with scarce financial and technological resources.
- Extended time required to establish themselves in the marketplace.
- Ongoing efforts to identify and recruit skilled personnel aligned with the company's mission and leadership style.

The primary objective of talent acquisition and retention is to facilitate sustainable growth and competitive advantage. Entrepreneurial firms seek to attract individuals possessing unique skills across various functional areas, including technical, managerial, and financial domains. These qualified candidates generally prefer established work environments offering ample personal and professional development opportunities. To address recruitment challenges, many companies rely on referrals and social media platforms like LinkedIn to connect with potential employees[6].

Quality Offering

Entrepreneurial ventures are created to offer goods and/or services to potential customers. The offering is the fundamental reason for their existence, driving long-term growth and market expansion. However, no offering should be accepted or marketed without carefully considering customer needs and expectations. Companies, therefore, must prioritize customer focus, including expectations around price, quality, delivery, and other aspects related to the offering. Consumers generally appreciate innovative, competitive, consistent, convenient, and safe products. They also value friendly, reliable, fast, and convenient services.

Entrepreneurial ventures can create sustainable competitive advantages and drive continuous growth by prioritizing customer-centric innovation and maintaining a long-term focus. Market research and consumer-focused groups are essential for understanding customer needs and desires for specific products or services. Customer needs analysis has become significantly easier due to technological advancements, particularly social media, analytics, and AI tools like ChatGPT, Google Gemini, and Microsoft Copilot.

---

[6] In an article titled The Most In-Demand Skills for 2024, Brodnitz, Dan indicated the following: Communication, customer service, leadership, project management, management, analytics, teamwork, sales, Problem-solving, and research. https://www.linkedin.com/business/talent/blog/talent-strategy/linkedin-most-in-demand-hard-and-soft-skills. Moreover, According to the Strada Education Foundation, the following skills are highly demanded by business firms: leadership, innovation, management, project management, customer service, communication, software development, operations, and problem-solving. Pelesh, Andrew (2018). The Top 10 Skills in Demand at Top 10 U.S. Companies. https://stradaeducation.org/employers/the-top-10-skills-in-demand-at-the-top-10-u-s-companies/

Core values

Company core values reflect the cultural value system, consisting of social and ethical beliefs and practices that distinguish the company from others. Leadership and employees must adhere to these core values and corresponding behaviors when dealing with customers, suppliers, and other stakeholders. Declared core values enhance the company's reputation and strengthen its market position. Moreover, Core values provide the ethical foundation for creating the company's vision, and the core value statement specifies the company's commitment to integrity, fairness, equal employment opportunity, accountability, and other exemplary attributes[7]. Entrepreneurial companies with socially admired core values can assist in obtaining critical resources such as talented employees, funds, and customer trust. The following is an example of core values: Excellence, inclusivity, integrity, accountability, and innovation (Bowie State University).

Continuous Improvement and Learning

A company's statement of continuous improvement declares excellence as essential for its survival, innovation, and growth. Progressive companies consistently strive to enhance their products, processes, and operations. They continually improve their performance to serve customers, employees, and the public. Entrepreneurial companies' continuous improvement practices bolster their resilience and foster learning (knowledge creation), leading to greater improvement and effectiveness[8]. Toyota, Boeing, McDonald's, and Microsoft are examples of companies known for continuous improvement efforts.

The fundamental sources of continuous improvement, which drive a firm's competitive advantage, are numerous and include:

- Visionary leadership
- Strategic planning and team performance
- Talent, technology, and teamwork

---

[7] David, Fred R. at el. (2024). *Strategic Management*, Hoboken: New Jersey, Pearson Education, Inc., p.44.
[8] See, for example, Kovach, Jaison V. et al (2014). Managerial Impacts of Learning and Continuous Improvement Practices, *Journal for Quality and Participation*, 37(2), 25-28.

- Accumulated knowledge gained through experience and learning from both successes and failures.

Efficient Operational Processes

Best organizational practices strive to achieve efficient operational processes, leading to lower costs, higher quality, increased output, and optimal work performance. Effective processes require careful planning, adequate employee training, the implementation of appropriate technology, a supportive work environment, and strong team building and leadership. Efficient operational processes contribute to a company's profitability and market growth.

How to Choose Your First Business Venture as a New Entrepreneur?

Starting a business in the United States, a free-market economy where entrepreneurs and companies can flourish with minimal government intervention can be both rewarding and challenging. As a legal entity, an established business carries responsibilities to customers, employees, government agencies, and other stakeholders. Therefore, carefully examining, assessing, and testing a new business idea is crucial for its viability.

To establish a potential business with growth and success, consider the following essential factors:

- Understand your technical and nontechnical skills, passion for entrepreneurship, willingness for risk-taking, dealing with people, stamina to work hard for long hours, and tolerance for failure.

- Assess the business idea for a product or service of your choice for its practicality. Undertake market research and learn about the potential demand for a similar offering. You may also consult with family members or close relatives and friends about the idea.

- List the kind and quantity of inputs needed for offering the desired output. This includes hardware, software, number of

- initial skilled and unskilled employees, supplies, workspace, means of transportation, etc.
- Decide on the business model to adopt. For example, will the business be online, in a physical location, or both?
- Estimate the total cost of managing the venture for at least a year.
- Compare the total cost for the venture with your own funds and other sources of finance.
- Sources of venture financing include personal funds, bank borrowing, credit card borrowing, and borrowing from friends and family members. During the initial stage of operations, it's almost impossible to access financing from such sources as venture capitalists or angel investors. The venture's business model, products, and/or services must generate sufficient demand and profits to compensate investors for supplying funds and expertise to new business ventures.
- Successful ventures must aim at providing innovative, demanded goods or services by deploying artificial intelligence-related technologies or other advanced technologies. Potential customers should view the offerings as unique, convenient, reasonably priced, and accessible.

Summary

Entrepreneurship has experienced a surge in recent years, with creative minds establishing innovative companies across various industries worldwide. Many successful global brands, including Microsoft, Dell, Amazon, and Tesla, owe their existence to visionary entrepreneurs. These companies have significantly contributed to economic growth by creating jobs and delivering cutting-edge products and services.

Entrepreneurship plays a crucial role in driving innovation and economic prosperity. It encompasses a career path, an activity, and a field of study, focusing on identifying and capitalizing on untapped economic opportunities through strategic thinking and resource allocation.

Entrepreneurs seek to discover or create new business opportunities, leading to new industries and economic sectors.

Entrepreneurs are venture creators, investors, and individuals whose business aspirations differ from ordinary individuals. Their success depends on various factors, including vision, strategies, leadership, and product/market knowledge. The venture's success is influenced by factors such as talent, funding, technology, network resources, and market conditions.

Entrepreneurs typically progress through career stages, from would-be entrepreneurs with ideas to experienced serial entrepreneurs. They engage in leadership, strategic planning, external relations, internal communication, and various skills development activities. Successful entrepreneurs master fundamental entrepreneurship principles, including visionary thinking, calculated risk-taking, talent acquisition strategies, quality offerings, core values, continuous improvement, and efficient operational processes.

To establish a successful venture, consider the following essential factors: Assess your skills, passion for entrepreneurship, risk tolerance, and work ethic. Thoroughly examine your business idea through market research and consultation. List all necessary inputs for your chosen product or service. Decide on your business model (e.g., online, physical location, or both). Estimate startup costs and compare them with available funding sources. Consider various financing options, including personal funds, bank borrowing, and credit card borrowing. Aim to provide innovative, demanded goods or services using advanced technologies. Ensure your offerings are unique, convenient, reasonably priced, and accessible.

Questions

1. What has been the recent trend in entrepreneurship globally?
2. How does entrepreneurship contribute to economic growth?
3. What are the core principles that guide entrepreneurs?
4. What does it take to establish aa business venture?

Appendix 1
Self-assessment Exercise

Do you consider yourself a would-be entrepreneur?

In answering the following questions, remember that the common attributes of successful entrepreneurs are the following:

- Clear business vision.
- Drive for independence, accomplishment, and success.
- Opportunity seeker and exploiter.
- Leadership quality.
- Problem-solver.
- Strategic thinking.
- Innovation.
- Risk-taking.
- Responsibility.

1. Do you consider yourself a would-be entrepreneur?

    a) Yes, definitely
    b) Maybe
    c) No, not really
    d) Undecided

2. How interested are you in starting your own business?

   a) Very interested
   b) Somewhat interested
   c) Not very interested
   d) Not at all interested

3. Have you ever thought about starting your own company?

   a) Often
   b) Occasionally
   c) Rarely
   d) Never

4. Do you enjoy taking risks in your personal or professional life?

   a) Yes, I thrive on risk
   b) Moderately
   c) Not very much
   d) Not at all

5. How comfortable are you with uncertainty and ambiguity?

   a) Very comfortable
   b) Somewhat comfortable
   c) Not very comfortable
   d) Not at all comfortable

6. Do you prefer to work independently or as a team?

   a) Prefer to work independently
   b) Work well in both settings
   c) Prefer to work in a team
   d) Strongly prefer to work in a team

7. How do you feel about responsibility for your own success/failure?

   a) I love being responsible for my own success/failure
   b) I'm comfortable with it
   c) It's okay, but I also appreciate support
   d) I'd rather not be responsible for it

8. Do you enjoy coming up with new ideas and solutions?

   a) Yes, I love brainstorming new ideas
   b) I enjoy it moderately
   c) It's okay, but it's not my favorite activity
   d) I prefer to follow established procedures

9. How do you handle setbacks or failures?

   a) I learn from them and move forward
   b) I'm somewhat resilient
   c) It's difficult, but I try to bounce back
   d) I tend to give up easily

10. Do you enjoy networking and building relationships in your field?

    a) Yes, I thrive on networking
    b) I enjoy it moderately
    c) It's okay, but it's not my favorite activity
    d) I prefer to work alone

11. How do you feel about financial risk?

    a) I'm willing to take calculated financial risks
    b) I'm somewhat comfortable with financial risk
    c) I prefer to minimize financial risk
    d) I avoid financial risk whenever possible

12. Do you enjoy strategic planning and goal-setting?

    a) Yes, I love developing plans and setting goals
    b) I enjoy it moderately
    c) It's okay, but it's not my favorite activity
    d) I prefer to focus on day-to-day tasks

13. How do you handle conflicting priorities and tight deadlines?

    a) I excel at managing multiple tasks efficiently
    b) I'm fairly good at it
    c) It can be challenging, but I manage
    d) It's very difficult for me

14. Do you enjoy problem-solving and finding creative solutions?

   a) Yes, I love solving complex problems
   b) I enjoy it moderately
   c) It's okay, but it's not my favorite activity
   d) I prefer straightforward tasks

15. How do you feel about delegating tasks to others?

   a) I'm comfortable delegating tasks effectively
   b) I'm somewhat comfortable with delegation
   c) It's difficult for me to delegate tasks
   d) I prefer to do everything myself

16. Do you enjoy public speaking and presenting ideas?

   a) Yes, I love speaking in front of groups
   b) I'm fairly comfortable with public speaking
   c) It's okay, but it's not my favorite activity
   d) I avoid public speaking when possible

17. How do you handle criticism or negative feedback?

   a) I welcome constructive criticism and use it to improve
   b) I'm somewhat open to feedback
   c) It's difficult for me to accept criticism
   d) I tend to become defensive when criticized

18. Do you enjoy learning new skills and expanding your knowledge?

   a) Yes, I love continuous learning
   b) I'm fairly enthusiastic about learning
   c) It's okay, but it's not my favorite activity
   d) I prefer to stick with what I know

19. How do you feel about working long hours, especially during startup phases?

   a) I'm willing to put in extra effort when needed
   b) I'm somewhat comfortable with long hours
   c) It can be challenging for me
   d) I prefer regular working hours

20. Do you enjoy taking initiative and leading others?[9]

a) Yes, I thrive in leadership roles
b) I'm fairly comfortable with leadership
c) It's okay, but it's not my favorite activity
d) I prefer to follow instructions

---

[9] Answers (1-5) b and (6-20) a. If you answered at least 80 percent of the questions correctly, you appear to enjoy the entrepreneurship career.

Chapter 2
Innovation: The Magical Engine

> "Creativity is thinking up new things.
> Innovation is doing new things."
>
> Theodore Levitt

Chapter Objectives

- To enhance understanding of the meaning of innovation.
- To differentiate between the concepts of innovation and creativity.
- To grasp the significance of innovation.
- To evaluate one's knowledge of innovation.

Innovative nations are distinguished by technological progress and influence at the international level. These countries are recognized for their economic strength and competitive edge at the national level. Within organizations, innovative entities are poised for enduring growth and profitability. Conversely, creative individuals are celebrated for their achievements and leadership roles. Notable examples of countries that have gained prominence through innovation include the United States, Japan, and Germany. In contrast, the roster of influential innovators over recent years features figures such as Jeff Bezos (of Amazon.com), Elon Musk (of TESLA), and Jensen Huang (of NVIDIA).

The Need for Self-innovation and Creativity

Self-innovation and creativity are the cornerstones of lifelong learning. These practices empower you to become more intelligent, empathetic, knowledgeable, and compassionate, fostering a sense of purpose and direction in your personal and professional life.

- Innovative individuals effectively harness their skills with creativity. These visionary, strategic thinkers are often highly successful.

- Innovative entrepreneurs identify and assess promising economic opportunities, capitalizing on them to achieve their goals.

- Creative entrepreneurs excel at finding and deploying crucial resources to establish for-profit or socially driven ventures. Their ventures are the driving force behind national growth and progress.

What's Innovation? What's Invention?

Many related definitions of innovation have been published. For example, Merriam-Webster The dictionary defines it as "a new idea, method, or device." the Cambridge Dictionary considers it "a new idea, design, product, etc." Innovation and invention are closely connected concepts. Dieffenbacher (2024)[10], for example, clarified the distinction between innovation and invention by stating that innovation differs from improvement in that it entails undertaking something fundamentally new rather than merely enhancing existing practices. In contrast, invention refers to the generation of an idea that possesses innovative potential; it represents the original development of a product or the initiation of a process, signifying its debut appearance.

---

[10] Dieffenacher, Stefan (January 17, 2024). Innovation vs Invention: Definition, Difference & Importance, https://digitalleadership.com/blog/innovation-vs-invention/#Innovation_Vs_Invention_Definitions.

Types of Innovation[11]

Innovation has been classified into several kinds:

- Product Innovation: This focuses on changes to product features.

- Marketing Innovation: This refers to how the product is promoted.

- Financial Innovation: This deals with modifications in financial transaction processes.

- Process Innovation: This typically involves significant changes to how a product is created.

- Business Model Innovation: This focuses on how the product is delivered to the customer.

- Digital and non-digital innovation: This encompasses digital and all other products.

- Disruptive Innovation: This could involve a combination of approaches, as discussed further in this chapter.

A Sample of Noteworthy Innovation

Over the past years, individuals, businesses, educational institutions, and government agencies have launched numerous innovations that have significantly contributed to economic and technological advancements, particularly in the United States. In 2009, According to the institution, knowledge at Wharton released a list of 30 groundbreaking innovations that have reshaped the world. The table on the following page outlines these innovations.

---

11 See, for example, Yongyi, Qu (2023). Digital Innovation: Organizational Foundation and Chinese Heterogeneity, *China Economist*, 18(3), 2-22; OECD (2005). Oslo Manual, the Measurement of Scientific and Technological Innovations.

Table 1
Notable 30 Innovations

Internet, Broadband, www (browser and html	Office software (spreadsheet, word processors
DNA testing and sequencing/human genome mapping	Non-invasive laser/robotic surgery
Online shopping/e-commerce/auctions (e.g., eBay)	Graphic user interface
Open-source software and services (e.g., Linux, Wikipedia)	RFID and application (e.g., EZ pass)
Magnetic Resonance Imaging (MRI)	Photovoltaic solar energy
Media file compression (e.g., jpgemp3)	Large-scale wind turbine
Digital photography	Liquid crystal display (LCD)
Social networking via the Internet	Antiretroviral treatment for AIDS
Microprocessors	Microfinance
PC/laptop computers	Fiber optics
GPS systems	Mobile phones
ATMs	Barcodes and scanners
E-mail	Stents
Light emitting diodes	Genetically modified plants
Biotech	SRAM flash memory

Source: Knowledge at Wharton, https://knowledge.wharton.upenn.edu/article/a-world-transformed-what-are-the-top-30inno.

Moreover, numerous innovations have surfaced during the past three decades, such as electric vehicles, digital streaming services like Netflix and Amazon Prime offering speedy delivery, ride-hailing applications like Lyft, video conferencing through Zoom, commission-free trading platforms like Robinhood and peer-to-peer accommodations via Airbnb.

Innovative Leaders: The Entrepreneurs

Entrepreneurs across the United States and worldwide have been instrumental in founding and growing businesses that offer innovative products and services, enhancing convenience and comfort for society. These trailblazers drive the entrepreneurial process, characterized by innovation, foresight, perseverance, proactive action, risk acceptance, and venture initiation. Therefore, what defines an entrepreneur? An entrepreneur establishes a new business amidst risk and unpredictability, aiming to generate profits and expansion by identifying substantial opportunities and evaluating requisite resources to leverage these opportunities effectively[12]. In addition to being viewed as a process, entrepreneurship is seen as a discipline that seeks to understand how opportunities are discovered, created, and exploited[13].

Country Ranking in Entrepreneurship

Around the globe, numerous countries strive to foster entrepreneurship among their citizens through various incentives, both financial and non-financial. Some countries exhibit higher levels of entrepreneurial activity than others. According to CEOWORLD Magazine, the following countries have been recognized as the top 20 entrepreneurial nations worldwide as of March 2024:

---

[12] Scarborough, Norman M. and Cornwell, Jeffery R. (2019). *Entrepreneurship and Small Business Management*, New York: NY, Pearson Education, Inc.
[13] Neck, Christopher P. et al. (2018). *Entrepreneurship*, Washinton, D.C., Sage Publications, Inc.

Table 2
Entrepreneurship Country Ranking, 2024

1. United States	2. Germany	3. United Kingdom	4. Israel
5. United Arab Emirates	6. Poland	7. Spain	8. Sweden
9. India	10. France	11. Australia	12. Estonia
13. Ireland	14. Malaysia	15. Saudia Arabia	16. South Korea
17. Canada	18. Philippines	19. Denmark	20. Switzerland

Source: CEOWORLD Magazine, https://ceoworld.biz/World's Most Entrepreneurial Countries, 2024

The Role of Innovative Entrepreneurs

Over the past decades, scholars have extensively discussed the pivotal role that innovative entrepreneurs play in society, as outlined below:

- Initiating and expanding business enterprises.

- Creating new products, services, systems, and processes.

- Efficiently delivering goods and services through creative business models.

- Generating income through strategic resource allocation.

- Serving as the driving force behind economic growth and development.

- Elevating living standards.

- Enhancing societal conditions regarding social, cultural, and educational environments.

The Innovation Ecosystem[14]

An ecosystem, as defined by the Merriam-Webster Dictionary, is a system composed of a community of living organisms interacting with their environment, particularly under natural conditions. Ecosystems influence various entities, objects, and processes. On a national scale, several factors shape the innovation ecosystem. These include educational institutions, government bodies, businesses, financial institutions, the current state of technology, access to funding, the nature and usefulness of the innovation, consumer demand for such innovations, and the innovators themselves. The entrepreneurial innovation ecosystem incorporates the above forces in addition to considering the entrepreneur, the innovative product, the intended market, the competitive environment, accessible resources, and the added value of the innovation.

Creativity

Cambridge Dictionary provides a brief, concise definition of creativity: "the ability to produce or use original and unusual ideas." Another way to view creativity is to say that creativity is the production of novel and useful ideas[15]. Many authors emphasize that creativity must present something different, new, or innovative as well as appropriate to the task at hand, that is, to be useful and relevant[16], and that creativity's value lies in its ability to facilitate the development of novel and effective solutions to problems that emerge due to change[17]. The sources of individual

---

[14] See, for example, Purbasari, Ratih et al. (2023). Mapping Actors in the Digital Innovation Ecosystem to Support Innovation in Digital Startup, *Review of Integrative Business and Economics Research*, 12(4), 134-148; Klimas,
Patrycja and Czakon, Wojciech (2022). Gaming innovation ecosystem: actors, roles and co-innovation processes,
Revie of Managerial Sciences, 16(7), 2213-2259; Myllyoja, Jouko et al. (2022). Strengthening futures-oriented agenda for building innovation ecosystems, *European Journal of Futures Research*, 10(1), 1-9.
[15] Amabile, Teresa M. (1996). Creativity and Innovation in Organization, Harvard Business School.
[16] Kaufman, James C. (2016). *Creativity 101*, Springer Publishing Company, LLC.
[17] Cropley, D. H. (2015). Promoting Creativity and Innovation in Engineering Education, *Psychology of Aesthetics, Creativity, and Arts*, 9(2), 161-171.

creativity are many and include the following[18]:

- Intellectual skills (abilities).
- Knowledge.
- Styles of thinking.
- Personality.
- Motivation.
- Anticipated rewards.
- Physical environment.
- Social environment.

Attributes of Creative Individuals

It is fascinating to explore the most apparent characteristics of creative individuals. Understanding creativity can motivate those aspiring to become creative contributors to society. To tackle this subject, J.P. Guilford outlined the following traits as common among many creative people:

Table 3
Attributes of Creative People

Flexibility	Fluency	Elaboration	Originality
Breadth of interest	Sensitivity	Curiosity	Independence
Action	Reflection	Concentration	Persistence
Commitment	Sense of humor	Expression of personality	-

Source: Guilford, J. P. (1973). *Characteristics of Creativity*, U.S. National Institute of Education

Many attributes mentioned earlier are characteristic of inventors and innovators because these individuals are pivotal in driving societal

---

[18] Sternberg, Robert J. (2006). The Nature of Creativity, *Creativity Research Journal*, 18(1), 87-98.

change and progress. On the other hand, it's interesting to observe that intelligence, referring to an individual's ability to analyze and reason, is deeply connected with creativity, which essentially centers on uniqueness and originality. Tina Fey, on the website geediting.com in June 2024, encapsulated the psychologists' perspective on the behavior indicative of a low level of intelligence, which encompasses the following attributes:

- Lack of curiosity.
- Frequent Procrastination.
- Poor listening skills.
- Lack of adaptability.
- Neglecting self-improvement.
- Overconfidence in one's knowledge.
- Ignoring different perspectives.
- Lack of self-awareness.

Creative Individuals Across Various Fields

Creative individuals are prevalent across numerous industries, sectors, companies, and educational institutions nationwide. They are evident in fields such as art, engineering, literature, economics, medicine, mathematics, and even circus performance, among countless other professions and human endeavors. The roster of creative individuals is extensive, featuring notable names like Albert Einstein, Adam Smith, Steve Jobs, Bill Gates, Mark Zuckerberg, Henry Ford, Elon Musk, William Shakespeare, Leonardo da Vinci, Pablo Picasso, Walt Disney, and Robert De Niro.

Summary

Innovation and invention, though interconnected, have distinct roles. Invention sparks the genesis of a new idea, often holding the innovation potential. Innovation takes many forms: product, marketing, financial, process, business model, digital/non-digital, and disruptive. Each addresses a unique aspect of bringing novelty to the market.

Throughout history, innovations have revolutionized economies and technologies. This progress is driven by individuals and organizations that embrace risk and transformation. Entrepreneurs play a pivotal role. They identify opportunities, utilize resources effectively, and pioneer new products, services, and business models that fuel economic growth and societal advancement.

Creativity, the cornerstone of innovation, thrives on generating original and unconventional ideas. It's essential for crafting innovative solutions to problems. Factors shaping creativity include intellectual abilities, knowledge, cognitive styles, personality traits, motivations, and environmental influences.

Questions

1. What is the significance of innovation to the national economy? Explain.

2. Do entrepreneurs qualify as innovators? Discuss.

3. What advantages does creativity bring to the workplace? Can you elaborate on this?

4. Is creativity something individuals are born with or developed over time? Justify your perspective.

Appendix 2
SELF-TEST QUESTIONS: INNOVATION[19]

Choose the option that best represents your viewpoint on each statement.

1. What is the primary characteristic of innovation?

    A. It involves creating something entirely new.
    B. It is about improving existing products or processes.
    C. It focuses solely on financial gains.
    D. It requires no risk-taking.

2. Which of the following statements best describes innovation?

    A. Innovation is only applicable in business contexts.
    B. Innovation is the introduction of changes that significantly benefit society.
    C. Innovation is strictly limited to technological advancements.
    D. Innovation does not require creativity.

3. How does innovation differ from invention?

    A. Innovation is the process of inventing something new.
    B. There is no difference; they are the same thing.
    C. Innovation involves applying inventions to solve problems.
    D. Innovation is always successful where invention fails.

---

[19] The correct answers are the following: 1(B), 2(B), 3(C), 4(D), 5(D), 6(A), 7(D), 8(D), 9(B), 10(C).

The Creative Entrepreneur

4. In what field might innovation be least likely to occur?

   A. Technology
   B. Education
   C. Art
   D. Sports

5. Which of the following is NOT a component of the innovation process?

   A. Idea Generation
   B. Implementation
   C. Evaluation
   D. Dissemination

6. True or False: Innovation often involves taking risks.

   A. True
   B. False

7. What role does failure play in the innovation process?

   A. Failure is never part of the innovation process.
   B. Every innovation starts with a failure.
   C. Failures should be avoided at all costs.
   D. Failures are learning opportunities.

8. Which of the following is NOT a barrier to innovation?

   A. Lack of resources
   B. Resistance to change
   C. Fear of failure
   D. All of the above

9. How can organizations foster a culture of innovation?

   A. By punishing failures
   B. By encouraging experimentation and learning from mistakes
   C. By focusing solely on profits
   D. By avoiding change altogether

10. What is the impact of innovation on society?

    A. It makes society less competitive.
    B. It leads to job losses.
    C. It improves living standards and quality of life.
    D. It causes social unrest.

Chapter 3
THE INNOVATIVE MINDSET

"My entire mindset is about getting better and growing."

Teddy Bridgewater

Chapter Objectives

- To investigate the types of mindsets.
- To delve into the core characteristics of an innovative mindset.
- To assess the scope of potential business opportunities.
- To establish a connection between a growth mindset and business opportunities

A classic tale of the mind's strength unfolds in a farmhouse nestled deep in the countryside of the United States. There lived a father, a mother, and their son, John. One warm summer day, John explored the family's age-worn barn. He navigated the labyrinth of farming tools and towering haystacks, his keen eyes meticulously scanning the area, his mind actively searching for anything intriguing. Suddenly, his attention snagged on an unusual section of the haystack. There, nestled within, lay an antique watch. Though scratched, its intricate design and the subtle etching of his father's initials on the back revealed it unmistakably as his. The watch had vanished years ago, prompting extensive, fruitless searches by his parents. What set John apart was his ability to see beyond the surface. His discovery of the watch highlights the value of unwavering focus and the power of intellect in tackling challenges. The story is a testament to the potency of a sharp mind and the insights gained from meticulous observation.

The Human Mind[20]

An intriguing system, the human mind has created groundbreaking inventions and innovations throughout history. This includes, among others, the invention of the wheel, the development of languages, the discovery of electricity, the advent of the Internet, and the emergence of artificial intelligence (AI). Each of these advancements represents a significant leap forward in human progress.

The mind is distinct from other living organisms due to its essential functions, which include learning, perception, communication, and creativity. These functions collectively contribute to the unparalleled functionality and uniqueness of the human mind. Learning is the mind's ability to acquire new knowledge, skills, and behaviors throughout an individual's lifespan. Perception is the capacity to interpret sensory information from the environment, enabling humans to understand and interact with the world around them.

Communication is fundamental to the human mind, conveying thoughts, feelings, and ideas through spoken, written, or gestural languages. Creativity represents the mind's innovative potential, allowing individuals to generate novel ideas, solutions, and expressions. Another remarkable function of the human mind is its ability to store memories, essentially encoded representations of past experiences. Information processing involves analyzing, synthesizing, and interpreting data from various sources.

Decision-making is closely tied to information processing, which entails evaluating options, weighing outcomes, and choosing courses

---

[20] See, for example, Jarvis, Amy L. et al. (2024). Evidence for a Multidimensional Account of Cognitive and Affective Theory of Mind: A StateTrace Analysis, *Memory & Cognition*, 52(3), 525-535; Härtel, Charmine E. J. et al. (2010). Heart versus Mind: The Functions of Emotional and Cognitive Loyalty, *Australian Marketing Journal*, 18(1), 1-7; Gick, Evelyn et al. (2001). F.A. Hayek's Theory of Mind and Theory of Cultural Evolution Revisited: Toward an Integrated Perspective, *Mind & Society*, 2(1), 149-162; Fodor, J. A. (1997). The representational Theory of Mind. *The American Behavioral Scientist*, 40(6), 829-841.

of action based on past experiences, current circumstances, and future goals. The mind's complexity is also characterized by emotions, which play a significant role in motivation, social bonding, and regulating physiological responses. Observation and absorption of language are integral to developing communication skills and a quiring knowledge. Finally, intelligence creation is a multifaceted process involving the integration of cognitive abilities, emotional understanding, and creative thinking. Intelligence manifests in various forms, including analytical reasoning, emotional intelligence, and practical problem-solving skills.

What's a Mindset?[21]

Authors have proposed numerous definitions of mindset, each highlighting a particular aspect of this concept. For instance, the APA Dictionary of Psychology describes it as "a state of mind that influences how individuals think about and subsequently engage in their goal-directed activities, potentially promoting or hindering optimal performance". Meanwhile, the Cambridge Dictionary offers a simpler definition: "a person's approach to thinking and their beliefs." Buchanan (2024) embarked on a research project analyzing 100 different definitions of mindset to pinpoint the main themes within each. The central themes of the definitions are illustrated in Table 1. Regardless of the nuances in a specific definition of mindset, an individual's mindset at any given time might involve contemplating or visualizing future or present scenarios, such as aspiring to become an entrepreneur or striving to execute a task flawlessly. Moreover, individuals' mindsets could affect many aspects of their lives, including learning, resiliency, relationships, and achievement.

---

[21] The mindset has received extensive discussions in recent years. See, for example, Harré, Michael and El-Tarifi, Husam (2024). Testing Game Theory of Mind Models for Artificial Intelligence, *Games*, 15(1), 1; Soemer, Alexander et al. (2024). Mind wandering May Both Promote and Impair Learning, *Memory & Cognition*, 52(2). 373-389; Hochnadel, Aaron and Finamore, Dora (2015). Fixed And Growth Mindset in Education and How Grit Helps Students Persist in The Face of Adversity, *Journal of Education Research*, 11(1).

Table 1

Selected Definitional Emphasis on Mindset

Attitude	System of beliefs	State of mind	Patterns of belief	Mental Paradigm
Mental attitude	Knowledge structure	Perceptive	A set of assumptions	Frame of reference
Psychological context	Way of Knowing	Mental model	Our philosophy	Frames of mind

Source: Buchanan, Ash (2024). What is mindset? 100 definitions from the field, https://doi.org/10.31234/osf. io/5xeqv

The Two Types of Mindsets[22]

Experts distinguish between two mindsets:

- **Fixed mindset:** This mindset is the belief that intelligence, talents, and abilities are inborn and unchangeable. People with a fixed mindset believe these attributes cannot be improved through effort.

- **Growth mindset:** Unlike a fixed mindset, a growth mindset believes intelligence, skills, and other personality attributes can be developed through education, training, and determination.

Examples of a Fixed Mindset

Numerous examples illustrate the personality traits of individuals with a fixed mindset in work, business, and educational environments, as shown in Table 2 on the following page:

---

[22] It is widely believed that Carol Dweck S. pioneered research in the field of fixed and growth mindsets in her 2006 publication entitled Mindset: The New Psychology of Success. New York: NY, Ballantine Books.

Table 2

Examples of a Fixed Mindset

Resisting change	Avoiding challenges	Low expectations	Low self-belief
Avoiding risks	Defensive Attitude	Dismissing feedback	Believing talent is innate
Avoiding asking for help	Avoiding social situations	Insisting on one way of doing things	Fearing failure
Giving up easily	Avoiding self-growth	Fearing the unknown	Limited efforts

Individuals with a fixed mindset are likely to encounter numerous hurdles in life. This static way of thinking can make it difficult for them to overcome challenges, build good relationships, and achieve success. However, individuals with a fixed mindset can transition towards a growth mindset by engaging in challenging tasks, learning from their errors, and being receptive to dialogue, and valuing feedback on their behaviors and interactions with others.

Examples of a Growth Mindset

Again, many examples illustrate the personality characteristics of individuals with growth mindset in a variety of environments, as shown in Table 3 on the following page:

Table 3

Examples of a growth mindset

Understanding that success comes with hard work	Appreciating the value of feedback	Being interested in learning new skills	Developing Leadership qualities
Welcoming challenges	Seeing failure as a unique opportunity to learn	Accepting criticism	Celebrating winning
Viewing effort as the road to improvement	discovering different learning styles	Knowing their strengths and weaknesses	Finding inspiration in others' success
Creating social networks	Believing in personal development	Having a vision for the future	Having self-awareness and empathy

Research Findings: The Impact of Mindset[23]

Authors have examined the influence of fixed and growth mindsets on individuals and organizations in several fields, including entrepreneurship, education, and general business, as summarized below:

Entrepreneurship. Growth-minded entrepreneurs are more likely to spot profitable opportunities, evaluate them thoroughly, and leverage them for greater profitability. They can propel a business venture forward through innovation by inspiring employees to take calculated risks and experiment freely without the dread of failure. Such an attitude fosters an atmosphere where novel ideas are embraced, and learning from errors is considered integral to the innovation process. Growth-minded

---
23 See, for example, Kouzes, Tae Kyung and Posner, Barry Z. (2019). Influence of managers' mindset on leadership behavior, *leadership & Organization Development Journal*, 40(8), 829-844; Keating, L. A., & Heslin, P. A. (2015). *The Potential Role of Mindsets in Unleashing Employee Engagement*. Human Resource Management Review, 25(4), 329-341; Haynie, J. M., Shepherd, D., Mosakowski, E., & Earley, P. C. (2010). A Situated Metacognitive Model of the Entrepreneurial Mindset. Journal of Business Venturing, 25(2), 217-229; Murphy, Mary J. and Dweck, Carol S. (2016). Mindsets shape consumer behavior, *Journal of Consumer Psychology*, 26(1), 127-136.

employees are expected to tackle problem-solving tasks innovatively, devising superior solutions within entrepreneurial endeavors.

Furthermore, entrepreneurs with a growth mindset tend to make prudent decisions, identifying opportunities with keen insight. They perceive challenges as chances to expand their knowledge and skills, potentially spawning groundbreaking business concepts and ventures. A growth mindset motivates entrepreneurs to delve into new markets and adjust their strategies according to feedback and evolving conditions. They place a high value on self-improvement and actively seek advice, feedback, and consultations.

Entrepreneurs with this mindset focus on continuous learning, adaptability, and collaboration to secure success and maintain competitiveness in the market. Additionally, it is widely held that those with a growth mindset are better equipped to navigate failures and reversals in their projects. They regard challenges and setbacks as invaluable lessons.

Business. As environments evolve, business leaders with a growth mindset are open to embracing new technologies, systems, and methodologies. These leaders are inclined to launch more innovative products and services to fulfill customer needs and maintain a competitive edge. They often employ successful strategies by analyzing their companies' strengths and weaknesses, facilitating profitability and long-term viability. Under the guidance of leaders with a growth mindset, employees become more motivated, dedicated, and inventive. Such leaders are adept at foreseeing and capitalizing on nascent market trends, and they typically enlarge their businesses through strategic initiatives like differentiation, integration, diversification, and outsourcing, expanding their human, financial, and technological resources.

Education. The influence of a growth mindset among educators, students, policy-makers, and staff members in an educational institution can have far-reaching and substantial effects on a country's educational system. This type of environment is more likely to experience the emergence of innovative graduate and undergraduate study programs, increased enrollment rates, and attractive physical settings. It may also lead to improvements in enrollment, registration, and other processes.

Students in such institutions are expected to learn faster, demonstrate better academic performance, and complete their programs in a timely manner. Moreover, these students may become role models for their fixed-mindset peers, inspiring them to exert greater academic effort and achieve better outcomes. Progressive academic institutions with a growth mindset are well-positioned to contribute to the country's technological advancement, economic growth, and overall prosperity.

Developing a Growth Mindset

Entrepreneurs and others can cultivate and maintain a growth mindset using various effective strategies and practices, such as:

- Expanding your talents, knowledge, and expertise in areas that interest you.
- Setting specific goals (targets, desired outcomes) to be accomplished within a designated timeframe. For instance, learning about venture financing sources within five weeks.
- Building a supportive network of friends and colleagues.
- Cultivating persistence in pursuing your objectives.
- Welcoming feedback, advice, and guidance.
- Seeking challenging tasks or projects.
- Celebrating your successes and achievements, no matter how small.
- Thinking ambitiously about business opportunities.
- Managing your emotions, stress, and feelings with great care.
- Broadening your understanding of the economy, economic sectors, technology, and competitive advantages through reading and research.

- Training yourself in self-leadership, leadership, and team management.
- Being action-oriented and taking calculated risks.

Summary

The human mind is an intricate system for groundbreaking inventions and innovations throughout history. These advancements highlight the human mind's unique capabilities, including learning, perception, communication, creativity, memory storage, information processing, decision-making, and the integration of cognitive abilities, emotional understanding, and creative thinking.

A fixed mindset views intelligence, talents, and abilities as innate and unchangeable, suggesting that improving these qualities is futile. Conversely, a growth mindset posits that intelligence and abilities can be developed over time through dedication and hard work. Fixed and growth mindsets significantly impact individuals across various domains, including entrepreneurship, education, and business.

Entrepreneurs with a growth mindset are more likely to innovate, take calculated risks, and view challenges as learning and skill-enhancement opportunities. Similarly, business leaders with a growth mindset are open to adopting new technologies and methodologies, fostering innovation and employee motivation. A growth mindset among educators and students leads to improved academic performance, innovative curriculum development, and a culture of continuous learning.

Cultivating a growth mindset involves setting specific goals, building a supportive network, welcoming feedback, seeking challenging tasks, celebrating successes, managing emotions, broadening knowledge, and practicing self-leadership. By adopting these strategies, individuals can enhance their abilities, resilience, relationships, and achievements, contributing to personal and professional growth.

Questions

1. What groundbreaking inventions and innovations have resulted from human ingenuity?

2. Explain the distinctions between fixed and growth mindsets and describe how they differ in their learning and personal development approaches.

3. In creating business ventures, what aspects should an entrepreneur with a growth mindset concentrate on to foster success and innovation?

4. Elaborate on the factors that contribute to the development of a fixed mindset and discuss the potential consequences of adopting such a mindset.

Appendix 3
SELF-TEST QUESTIONS: FIXED VERSUS GROWTH MINDSET

Choose the option that best represents your viewpoint on each statement.

Question Set 1: Learning and Intelligence

1. How do you view your intelligence?

   A) It's something you're born with and can't change.
   B) It's something you can develop through dedication and hard work.
   C) It's a combination of both.
   D) It doesn't matter; everyone has equal potential.

2. What does it mean if someone says you did a great job but warns you to keep trying harder?

   A) You're doing well but must prove yourself further.
   B) You're doing well, and there's no need to improve.
   C) You're doing poorly and need to try harder.
   D) You're doing poorly and shouldn't bother trying.

3. Do you believe that talent alone makes people successful?

   A) Yes, talent is everything.
   B) No, talent is just the starting point.
   C) Yes, but only if you work hard.
   D) No, hard work is what matters.

4. How do you react to criticism?

   A) I take it personally and feel threatened.
   B) I see it as a chance to learn and grow.
   C) I ignore it.
   D) I become defensive and argue against it.

Question Set 2: Effort and Persistence

5. What does the phrase "you can't teach new tricks" suggest about learning?

   A) It suggests that older people cannot learn new things.
   B) It suggests that once learned, skills cannot be changed.
   C) It suggests that learning is easy for everyone.
   D) It suggests that persistence is futile.

6. How do you respond to failure?

   A) I give up; it's too difficult.
   B) I learn from it and try again.
   C) I blame others.
   D) I avoid situations that might lead to failure.

7. What does the idea of "fixed traits" suggest about abilities?

   A) Abilities are unchangeable.
   B) Abilities can be improved with effort.
   C) Abilities are determined by genetics.
   D) Abilities are influenced by luck.

8. How do you handle setbacks?

   A) I see them as insurmountable obstacles.
   B) I view them as opportunities to learn.
   C) I avoid acknowledging them.
   D) I become angry and frustrated.

Question Set 3: Challenges and Effort

9. What does the idea of "effort equals ability" suggest about intelligence?

   A) If you're smart, you'll succeed easily.
   B) If you're not smart, no amount of effort will help.
   C) Both effort and ability contribute to success.
   D) Only effort counts.

10. How do you approach challenging tasks?

    A) I avoid them; they're too hard.
    B) I tackle them head-on, believing I can master them.
    C) I procrastinate until the last minute.
    D) I delegate them to someone else.

11. What does the phrase "I'm not good at math" imply about your ability to improve?

    A) It means you're incapable of improving.
    B) It means you're willing to try but doubt your chances of success.
    C) It means you're open to learning and improving.
    D) It implies you're lazy.

Question Set 4: Feedback and Improvement

12. How do you interpret praise for your efforts?

    A) I feel uncomfortable and question its sincerity.
    B) I appreciate it and feel motivated to continue.
    C) I dismiss it, thinking it's unnecessary.
    D) I accept it but don't let it affect my future actions.

13. What does the idea of "natural talent" suggest about your abilities?

    A) Your abilities are predetermined and unchangeable.
    B) Your abilities can be enhanced with effort.
    C) Your abilities are solely based on innate gifts.

D) Your abilities are shaped by both nature and nurture.

14. How do you react to receiving feedback?

   A) You feel criticized and defensive.
   B) You seek ways to apply the feedback positively.
   C) You ignore the feedback.
   D) You feel grateful and motivated to improve.

15. What does the concept of "growth mindset" suggest about learning?

   A) Learning is effortless and comes naturally.
   B) Learning requires consistent effort and resilience.
   C) Learning is only for those who are naturally gifted.
   D) Learning is pointless since life outcomes are predetermined.

Based on the information provided in the chapter, the correct answers are the following:

Question Set 1: Learning and Intelligence

1. B) It's something you can develop through dedication and hard work.

2. B) You're doing well, and there's no need to improve.

3. B) No, talent is just the starting point.

4. B) It is a chance to learn and grow.

Question Set 2: Effort and Persistence

5. A) It suggests that older people cannot learn new things.

6. B) I learn from it and try again.

7. B) Abilities can be improved with effort.

8. B) I view them as opportunities to learn.

Question Set 3: Challenges and Effort

9. C) Both effort and ability contribute to success.

10. B) I tackle them head-on, believing I can master them.

11. C) It means you're open to learning and improving.

Question Set 4: Feedback and Improvement

12. B) I appreciate it and feel motivated to continue.

13. B) Your abilities can be enhanced with effort.

14. B) You seek ways to apply the feedback positively.

15. B) Learning requires consistent effort and resilience.

Chapter 4
Self-Innovation

"Do the best you can until you know better.
Then, when you know better, do better."

Maya Angelou

Chapter Objectives

- To understand the core meaning of the self-innovation concept.

- To become proficient in the essential elements that enable self-innovation.

- To learn how to effectively apply the knowledge acquired about the concept into learning and practical applications.

- To identify and establish the connections between self-innovation, self-leadership, and self-reliance.

Entrepreneurship propels economic growth and technological advancement within a free, open economy like the United States. It is an engaging domain for professional and academic exploration and a hands-on arena for initiating new businesses, generating employment opportunities, and introducing novel products and services. As entrepreneurship increasingly permeates even nations with traditionally closed economies under strict government control over trade and financial activities, its inherent nature requires entrepreneurs—both novice and experienced—to embody qualities of self-innovation to thrive and expand their enterprises. Would-be entrepreneurs must be prepared to develop entrepreneurial abilities, managerial competencies, a growth-oriented mindset, and visionary leadership, distinguishing themselves from individuals with a fixed mindset who lack these entrepreneurial traits.

What's Self-innovation?[24]

In this book, the term "self-innovation" is employed within the framework of entrepreneurship discussions to denote the process or action of innovating oneself. This entails creating or reinstating one's skills, knowledge, or other attributes to accommodate evolving situations or foster personal advancement. Self-innovation emphasizes individuals prioritizing their own development and adaptation to instigate and steer change within their entrepreneurial ventures or personal spheres. It encompasses innovation in capability, talent enhancement, and strategic thinking to navigate better and impact their surroundings. On the other hand, the concept of *self-invention* is defined as "the act or instance of inventing or creating one's identity or conception of oneself" (Meriam-Webster Dictionary) and the process of creating your own identity, who you are and the quality that makes different from others (Cambridge Dictionary).

Self-innovation represents a transformative process through which individuals elevate their mindset, talents, and vision to a superior level of knowledge, expertise, and insight. This journey demands significant effort and activity, consuming most of one's time and resources. Despite the challenges and obstacles encountered along the way, the benefits of such transformation often significantly surpass its difficulties. Self-innovation is the ultimate goal for those seeking self-leadership, self-reliance, and self-satisfaction. It is particularly prevalent among those destined to become serial entrepreneurs. These individuals are committed to continuous learning and applying innovative strategies to propel their businesses forward with unwavering determination and creativity.

---

[24] See, for example, Jason, Jaggard, Mastering the Art of Self-Innovation, *Global Leadership Network*, https://globalleadership.org/articles/leading-yourself/mastering-the-art-of-self-innovation;

Manacha (2023) indicated that the innovative attitude declares that[25]:

- I will learn.
- I will seek.
- I will question.
- I will be aware.
- I will observe.
- I will choose.
- I can.
- I am open.

The self-innovation list could be expanded to encompass the following:

- I can innovate my habits, communication, and relationships.
- I commit to reading, learning, and exploring new avenues of opportunity.
- I strive to think creatively beyond the present moment, the immediate day, and the superficial aspects.
- I aim to confront and overcome timidity.
- With a growth mindset, I believe I can achieve my goals.
- I possess the ability to manage my emotions effectively.
- I value both myself and others.
- I am open to accepting constructive criticism and feedback.

---

[25] Manacha, Sailaja (2023). Self-innovation for Leaders – A Tool Supporting Leading by Influence, (www.hptts://sailajamanacha.com).

The Genesis of Self-innovation

The origin of self-innovation theory dates back to several decades of scholarly contributions, discussions, and theories. It's commonly believed that the following theories are the backbone of the self-innovation theories:

- Self-Determination Theory (SDT).
- Growth Mindset Theory (GMT).
- Social Cognitive Theory (SCT).
- Transformational Learning (Leadership) Theory (TLT).
- Theory of Planned Behavior (TPB).
- Self-Efficacy Theory (SET).
- Self-Leadership Theory (SLT).
- Experiential Learning Theory (ELT).
- Diffusion of Innovation Theory (DIT).
- Complexity Theory (CT).

This chapter addresses four of the most widely discussed theories: Self-Determination Theory, Social Cognitive Theory, Self-Efficacy Theory, and Diffusion of Innovation Theory. The dominant concepts among these theories are human behavior, motivation, and action, as summarized below:

Self-Determination Theory (SDT)[26]

The Self-Determination Theory suggests a psychological perspective on human nature, focusing on the intrinsic motivations that drive individuals. This theory emphasizes three fundamental psychological

---

[26] See, for example, Gagné, Maryléne and Deci, Edwards S. (2005). Self-determination theory and work motivation, *Journal of Organizational Behavior*, 26(4). 331; Pitchary, Anwar A. et al. (2022). Self-determination theory and individuals' intention to participate in donation crowdfunding, *International Journal of Islamic and Middle Eastern Finance and Management*, 15(3), 506-526.

needs: autonomy, competence, and relatedness. These needs are crucial for fostering personal development and psychological well-being. When these basic needs are satisfied, individuals are more inclined to pursue growth and realize their full potential.

Autonomy encompasses the desire to self-govern one's behaviors, goals, and life path. Competence involves the aspiration to be efficacious and competent in one's endeavors. Relatedness pertains to the longing for social connections and nurturing interpersonal relationships. The theory suggests that individuals are more likely to act when they believe their actions influence outcomes, enhancing their motivation. Meeting the core needs of autonomy, competence, and relatedness is instrumental in advancing personal growth, adaptability, and flexibility.

Social Cognitive Theory (SCT)[27]

The theory offers an insightful framework for understanding how individuals learn from others and their external environment by believing in their capabilities and talents to achieve success. This framework comprises several pillars, including reciprocal determinism, which explores the mutual influence of the environment on individuals and their influence on the environment; self-efficacy, referring to a person's belief in their ability to accomplish tasks; modeling, the process through which individuals learn by observing others as role models; and reinforcement, which involves internal and external responses determining whether a particular behavior is repeated or not. Additionally, the theory stresses the importance of attention, retention, and motivation in the learning process.

---

[27] See, for example, Ratten, Vanessa and Ratten, Hamish (2007). Social Cognitive Theory in Technological Innovations *European Journal of Innovation Management*, 10(1), 90-108; Mazahem, Najib A. (2022). Social cognitive theory and women's career choices: an agent-based model simulation, *Computational and Mathematical Organization Theory*, 28(1), 1-26.

Self-Efficacy Theory (SET)[28]

The Self-Efficacy Theory is closely linked to the previously discussed Social Cognitive Theory. It emphasizes an individual's confidence in their capabilities, including their skills, talents, and the ability to exert the necessary effort to attain specific goals or achieve desired outcomes. Individuals with high self-efficacy often pursue ambitious and time-intensive objectives, such as becoming proficient in the science of artificial intelligence (AI). This theory plays a crucial role in shaping an individual's efforts, actions, resolve, and motivation toward achieving their goals. Various elements influence an individual's self-efficacy, including successfully overcoming difficult challenges, witnessing others' achievements, receiving support and encouragement from others, and maintaining a positive mindset and relaxed state.

Diffusion of Innovation Theory (DIT)[29]

The Diffusion of Innovation Theory is a framework within social sciences that elucidates the mechanisms through which new products, services, ideas, technologies, or other forms of innovation disseminate across communities and cultures, both domestically and internationally. This theory holds particular significance in areas such as entrepreneurship and corporate environments. At its core, DIT posits that adopting innovations is contingent upon various factors, including the advantages they offer, their complexity, and their alignment with existing innovations and societal norms and customs.

---

[28] See, for example, Ngulube, V. B. and Ogbonnaya, Ijeoma C. (2023). Applying Bandura's Theory of Self-Efficacy to Assess the Perceptions of Pre-service Economics Teachers Concerning Reaching using Graphs, *International Journal in Business and Social Science*, 12(8), 517-525; Alverez-Huerta, Paula et al. (2022). Entrepreneurial self-efficacy among first-year undergraduates: Gender, creative self-efficacy, leadership self-efficacy, and field of study, *Entrepreneurial Business and Economics Review*, 10(4), 37-89.

[29] See, for example, Lundberg, Mary et al. (2019). Diffusion of innovation in a contractor company: The impact of the social system structure on the implementation process, *Construction Innovation*, 19(4), 629-652; Karmanov, Mikhail V. et al. (2020). The Process of Innovation Diffusion and Adoption of Innovations in the Business Modelling for Travel Companies, *Journal of Environmental Management & Tourism*, 11(2), 346-354.

According to this theory, the adaptation process begins once individuals become cognizant of the innovation, express interest in it, and assess its merits through trial and error. DIT categorizes adapters into five groups:

- Innovators: Individuals who are keen on exploring novel concepts.
- Early Adopters: Those willing to embrace new ideas.
- Early Majority: Individuals who surpass the average rate of adoption.
- Late Majority: People who adopt innovations only after the majority has done so.
- Laggards: A minority group characterized by resistance to change.

The Psychology of Entrepreneurship[30]

People engage in entrepreneurship for various reasons, influenced by differing environmental contexts and cultural backgrounds. Entrepreneurship psychology, a subfield within psychology, explores the mental states and emotional inclinations of those who seek to capitalize on profitable prospects or achieve societal objectives through starting new ventures. External factors play significant roles in shaping individual decisions to become entrepreneurs. The factors include the following:

- National culture,
- Economic conditions of the country,
- The individuals' professional paths,

---

[30] See, for example, Omorede, Adesuwa et al. (2015). Entrepreneurship psychology: a review, *International Entrepreneurial and Management Journal*, 11(4), 743-768; Grigore, Ana-Maria (2012). The Psychology of Entrepreneurship, *Romanian Journal of Marketing*, 2, 25-36; Salmony, Florentine and Ranbach, Dominik K. (2022). Personality trait differences across types of entrepreneurs: a systematic literature review, *Review of Management Science*, 16(3), 713-749. Frese, Michael and Gielnik, Michael (2023). The Psychology of Entrepreneurship: Action and Process, *Annual Review of Organizational Psychology and Organizational Behavior*, 10, 137-164, https://doi.org/10.1146/annurev-orgpsych-120920-055546.

- Governmental policies regarding entrepreneurship and business,
- Access to venture capital and
- The country's levels of unemployment.

The table below outlines the primary characteristics of entrepreneurs, as identified by researchers in the field of entrepreneurship:

Table 1

The Psychology of Entrepreneurship

Self-efficacy	Vision	Opportunity seeker
Need for achievement	Self-confidence	Adaptability
Risk-taking	Strategic thinking	Persistence
Goal oriented	Ability to influence outcomes (locus of control)	Enthusiastic
Motivation	Need for financial independence	Innovativeness

Source: Various sources.

Summary

Self-Innovation: In entrepreneurship, self-innovation refers to continually renewing and enhancing one's skills, knowledge, and attributes to adapt to changing circumstances and achieve personal growth. It involves prioritizing self-development and strategic thinking to navigate and impact one's environment effectively. This process is transformative, requiring significant effort but yielding substantial rewards in self-leadership, self-reliance, and self-satisfaction.

Key Attitudes for Self-Innovation:

- Commitment to learning and exploration
- Creative thinking beyond immediate concerns
- Overcoming timidity and managing emotions

- Valuing oneself and others
- Accepting constructive criticism and feedback

Origins of Self-Innovation Theory: Self-innovation theory draws from several established theories, particularly in the field of psychology:

- Self-Determination Theory (SDT): Focuses on intrinsic motivations driven by needs for autonomy, competence, and relatedness.
- Social Cognitive Theory (SCT): Emphasizes learning from the environment and believing in one's capabilities (self-efficacy).
- Self-Efficacy Theory (SET): Highlights confidence in one's abilities to achieve goals.
- Diffusion of Innovation Theory (DIT): Explains how innovations spread through societies, categorizing adopters into innovators, early adopters, early majority, late majority, and laggards.

Psychology of Entrepreneurship: Entrepreneurial motivation is influenced by various factors, including cultural, economic, and political environment. Key characteristics of entrepreneurs include self-efficacy, vision, opportunity-seeking, adaptability, risk-taking, strategic thinking, persistence, and a need for achievement and independence.

Self-innovation is a critical component of entrepreneurial success, requiring a growth-oriented mindset and the continuous development of skills and capabilities. Various psychological and behavioral theories support this process, highlighting the importance of motivation, learning, and adaptability in entrepreneurship.

Questions

1. Explain the concept of self-innovation.
2. What are the methods individuals can use to enhance their self-innovation?

3. Identify the sources of self-innovation.
4. Discuss some psychological characteristics of entrepreneurs.

Chapter 5

CULTIVATING PERSONAL GROWTH FOR ENTREPRENEURIAL SUCCESS

> "The swiftest way to triple your success is to double your investment in personal development."
>
> Robin Sharma

Chapter Objectives

- To understand the importance of personal growth.
- To identify key areas for personal development.
- To develop strategies for self-improvement.
- To integrate personal growth into business practices

Distinguishing itself from other professional fields like education, medicine, and law, entrepreneurship focuses on uncovering, leveraging, and expanding market opportunities. This pursuit is crucial for fostering national and global economic growth and sustainability. Entrepreneurs are the innovators behind creative concepts and initiatives, leading the charge in introducing new and improved products and services. They secure funding to support their endeavors, efficiently allocate resources, drive technological advancements, and positively impact societal issues. To succeed in an entrepreneurial career, an individual must develop and enhance the psychological attributes of accomplished entrepreneurs, such as strategic thinking, self-efficacy, a willingness to take calculated risks, and visionary planning, to mention a few.

What's Personal Growth?

Authors frequently interchange the terms personal growth, self-improvement, and personal development. The APA Dictionary defines personal growth as "the growth or improvement of one's qualities and abilities." Expanding on this definition, personal growth can involve various aspects such as an individual's values, technical and non-technical skills, beliefs, thought processes, vision, behavior, actions, emotions, habitual practices, and future outlook. Personal growth aims at achieving self-actualization and realizing one's full potential, encompassing an individual's life.

Benefits of Personal Growth[31]

Experts in the fields of psychology and human resource management, among others, have discussed the significance and advantages of personal growth. Their findings indicate that engaging in personal growth activities provides individuals with a wide range of benefits, encompassing mental, physical, spiritual, and emotional aspects, as summarized table 1 on the following page:

---

[31] See, for example, 10 Most Profound Benefits of Personal Growth, www.https//strengtheatre-com.medium.com;
Beutell, Nicholas et al. (2019). A look at the dynamics of personal growth and self-employment exit, *International Journal of Entrepreneurial Behavior Research*, 25(7), 1452-1470; Baek-Kyoo (Brian), Joo et al. (2021). Personal growth initiative: the effects of person-organization fit, work empowerment and authentic leadership, *International Journal of Manpower*, 42(3), 502-517; Toyama, Masahiro et al. (2020). Psychosocial Factors Promoting Personal Growth Throughout Adulthood, *Journal of Happiness Studies*, 21(5), 1749-1769.

Table 1

Benefits of Personal Growth

Expanding mental capacity	Increasing probability for goal-achievement	Improving communication	Becoming a better thinker
Enhancing knowledge and expertise	Improving relationships with others	Becoming self-aware	Gaining self-resilience
Opening new windows of opportunities	cultivating creativity	Improving self-confidence	Improving decision-making
Adapting to change	Gaining a greater sense of direction	Strengthening the mindset	Setting attainable goals

Sources: Various sources.

Planning for Self-growth

Effective planning is a systematic process. It involves interconnected activities culminating in an action plan to achieve desired goals or objectives. This process unfolds in distinct stages.

- Stage 1: Environmental assessment. This stage begins with assessing the environment, which includes internal and external factors.

- Internal assessment (Self-assessment): This involves understanding oneself by identifying strengths and weaknesses. The aim is to leverage these strengths and address weaknesses to foster personal growth. The assessment should target key life aspects, such as general and career-specific education, emotional intelligence, communication skills, leadership abilities, critical thinking, and self-creativity.

- External assessment: This component focuses on gaining insights into the external demands placed upon you and the surrounding environment. It covers areas such as required skills, vision alignment, knowledge gaps, communication needs, and resources required.

- Stage 2: Goal setting: Based on the internal and external assessments, this stage involves creating what is often called SMART goals (Specific, Measurable, Achievable, Relevant, and Time-bound).

- Stage 3: Resource allocation and efforts: This stage involves organizing a schedule of activities, specifying the required time, type of effort, and other resources necessary to meet the established goals.

- State 4: Follow up periodically (e.g., monthly) and adjust the plan as needed.

For individuals to achieve self-growth, they must embrace change, welcome feedback, seek inspiration, explore available support systems, align their strengths with external opportunities, demonstrate resilience, and prioritize their physical well-being.

Entrepreneurial Essential Competencies

Individuals choosing entrepreneurial paths need to cultivate more personal growth in business and economics than those headed toward other professions like software development, accounting, or teaching art. As discussed elsewhere in this book, entrepreneurship focuses on identifying and leveraging opportunities through creating and expanding businesses for profit or social impact. Engaging in entrepreneurial endeavors requires proficiency in several key areas:

- Leadership and management duties.
- Understanding industry, market, and economic trends.
- Securing venture capital.
- Identifying target customers' needs.
- Expertise in products or services offered.
- Strategic planning methodologies.

- Building and utilizing business networks.
- Focusing on product improvement and innovation.
- Exploring different business models.
- Exploring opportunities via professional networking and market research.

Theories on Creativity and Innovation

Scholars specializing in the realms of creativity and innovation have put forth numerous compelling theories focused on fostering personal growth and enhancing effectiveness. According to the Britannica Dictionary, creativity is "the capacity to create new things or conceive novel ideas, whereas innovation is "the action or process of bringing forth new ideas, devices, or techniques." These definitions underscore the interconnectedness of creativity and innovation, centered around generating fresh ideas, problem-solving, and surmounting obstacles.

These concepts are pivotal in an individual's development and advancement, serving as foundational elements for national economic and technological progress. However, it's important to note that while individuals often serve as the primary sources of creativity, innovation tends to emerge from collaborative efforts. Creativity can sometimes appear abstract and devoid of immediate applications, like envisioning space travel without the technology to support it. Conversely, innovation is typically characterized by its practicality and tangible results, such as the creation of the electric car. The core principles of creativity and innovation encompass the following:

- **Generating new ideas:** Creativity and innovation involve creating original concepts and solutions.
- **Problem-solving:** They are instrumental in addressing and resolving issues through innovative approaches.
- **Overcoming challenges:** Individuals can overcome seemingly insurmountable obstacles by thinking creatively and innovatively.

Summary

Entrepreneurship distinguishes itself from traditional professions by focusing on discovering, utilizing, and expanding market opportunities, playing a vital role in economic growth and sustainability. Entrepreneurs, as innovators, introduce new products and services, secure financing, manage resources efficiently, advance technology, and address societal issues. Success in entrepreneurship hinges on developing psychological traits such as strategic thinking, risk-taking, and visionary planning.

Personal growth involves enhancing one's qualities and abilities, including values, skills, beliefs, behaviors, and future outlook, aiming for self-actualization. Experts highlight the mental, physical, spiritual, and emotional benefits of engaging in personal growth activities. Effective self-growth planning involves assessing the environment (both internal and external), setting SMART goals, allocating resources, and conducting periodic follow-ups. Embracing change, seeking feedback, and prioritizing well-being are crucial for personal growth.

Entrepreneurs must excel in leadership, market understanding, securing capital, identifying customer needs, product/service expertise, strategic planning, and network building. These skills are essential for navigating the complexities of starting and growing a business. Creativity and innovation are intertwined, emphasizing the generation of new ideas, problem-solving, and overcoming challenges. While creativity may seem abstract, innovation is practical and leads to tangible outcomes. Both are fundamental to individual development and national progress, with innovation often emerging from collaboration.

In essence, entrepreneurship and personal growth are interrelated, requiring a high level of personal development in areas such as leadership, innovation, and strategic planning. Personal growth, in turn, fosters creativity and innovation, which are crucial for both individual success and societal advancement.

Questions

1. What is the role of creativity and innovation in entrepreneurship?
2. How can personal growth contribute to entrepreneurial success?
3. What strategies can leaders employ to enhance employee creativity and innovation?
4. How do creativity and innovation work together in the entrepreneurial process?

Appendix 4

SELF-TEST QUESTIONS: CULTIVATING PERSONAL GROWTH FOR ENTREPRENEURIAL SUCCESS:

Instructions: Choose the best answer for each question.

1. Which of the following is NOT a key benefit of personal growth for entrepreneurs?

    a) Increased knowledge and skills.
    b) Improved ability to manage stress.
    c) Reduced workload and responsibility.
    d) Enhanced problem-solving capabilities.

2. Entrepreneurs who embrace a growth mindset believe that:

    a) Their intelligence and abilities are fixed.
    b) Challenges are opportunities to learn and grow.
    c) Failure is a sign of weakness.
    d) Success comes naturally without effort.

3. A good way to cultivate a passion for learning is to:

    a) Only focus on acquiring skills directly related to your business.
    b) Actively seek out new knowledge and experiences.
    c) Avoid challenges and unfamiliar situations.
    d) Delegate all learning opportunities to others.

4. Setting SMART goals for personal growth helps to ensure they are:

    a) Open-ended and flexible.

b) Specific, Measurable, Achievable, Relevant, and Time-bound.
c) Vague and aspirational.
d) Based on other people's expectations.

5. Building a strong network can benefit entrepreneurs by:

    a) Creating a sense of isolation.
    b) Providing access to valuable resources and support.
    c) Limiting opportunities for independent thinking.
    d) Increasing competition within the industry.

6. Regularly reflecting on your progress allows you to:

    a) Dwell on past mistakes.
    b) Identify areas for improvement.
    c) Ignore challenges you haven't overcome yet.
    d) Become complacent with your current achievements.

7. When faced with setbacks, entrepreneurs with high resilience are likely to:

    a) Give up easily and abandon their goals.
    b) Learn from their mistakes and try again.
    c) Blame others for their failures.
    d) Avoid taking risks altogether.

8. Prioritizing your well-being as an entrepreneur includes:

    a) Working long hours without breaks.
    b) Maintaining a healthy balance between work and personal life.
    c) Neglecting your physical and mental health needs.
    d) Sacrificing sleep for productivity.

9. Effective time management for entrepreneurs involves:

    a) Procrastinating on important tasks.
    b) Prioritizing tasks based on urgency and importance.
    c) Trying to do everything at once.
    d) Avoiding delegating tasks to others.

10. Effective communication skills are essential for entrepreneurs because they allow them to:

    a) Talk down to their customers and employees.
    b) Clearly convey their ideas and vision.
    c) Ignore feedback and suggestions from others.
    d) Be overly critical and judgmental.

11. When seeking feedback on your business ideas, it's best to:

    a) Only listen to positive comments.
    b) Consider constructive criticism to improve.
    c) Take offense at any negative feedback.
    d) Avoid seeking feedback from others altogether.

12. Adaptability is a key skill for entrepreneurs because it allows them to:

    a) Resist change and cling to outdated methods.
    b) Adjust their strategies in response to new challenges.
    c) Ignore market trends and customer preferences.
    d) Be inflexible and unwilling to learn new things.

13. Entrepreneurs who are lifelong learners are more likely to:

    a) Become stagnant and uninspired.
    b) Stay ahead of the competition and industry trends.
    c) Resist opportunities for professional development.
    d) Be satisfied with a limited skill set.

14. Reading industry publications and attending workshops are examples of which type of personal growth activity?

    a) Building relationships.
    b) Continuous learning.
    c) Time management improvement.
    d) Stress management techniques.

15. Regularly taking time for self-reflection can help you identify your:

   a) Weaknesses and areas for improvement.
   b) Competition within your industry.
   c) Most profitable business opportunities.
   d) The best employees to hire.

Correct answers:

1(d), 2-14 (b), 15(a).

Chapter 6
INSIGHTS INTO CREATIVITY THEORIES

"The worst enemy to creativity is self-doubt."

Sylvia Plath

Chapter Objectives

- To identify key creativity theories.
- To understand the importance of creativity theories.
- To be able to evaluate creativity theories critically.
- To learn how to utilize creativity theories

Since the publication of Graham Wallas's seminal work, "The Art of Thought,"[32] in 1926, the subject of the creative process, widely recognized by many psychologists as the cradle of innovation, has seen growing attention from educators and researchers alike. In his book, Wallas introduced the concept that an individual's creative journey evolves through four distinct yet interrelated stages when confronted with problem-solving scenarios. Initially, one identifies issues and gathers pertinent information (preparation phase); subsequently, one delves deeply into the matter at hand (incubation phase); then, innovative ideas emerge (illumination phase); finally, these new ideas are assessed, and alternative solutions are explored (verification phase). Wallas's insights into creativity resonate with modern approaches

---
[32] https://archive.org/details/theartofthought.

to problem-solving, which are prevalent in educational contexts and applied broadly across industries.

Assessing Creativity[33]

Educators, psychologists, and other professionals have devised numerous assessments to gauge creativity, especially among students and the labor force. These evaluations uncover individuals' aptitude for problem-solving and overcoming obstacles across various settings, such as workplaces. One of the most commonly employed tests, introduced by Ellis Paul Torrance in the mid-20th century, is the Torrance Tests of Creative Thinking. This assessment pinpoints crucial elements of creativity through four primary domains:

- Fluency: This metric assesses the individual's capability to produce a variety of ideas, interpretations, or perspectives in reaction to a particular scenario, item, or issue.

- Flexibility: It measures the individual's ability to generate various responses, showcasing a broad spectrum of cognitive strategies.

- Originality: This aspect emphasizes the novelty of the person's ideas.

- Elaboration: It assesses the depth and complexity of the individual's response.

The Torrance Tests imply that creativity arises from a mix of intrinsic qualities. Nonetheless, the author acknowledges the impact of external surroundings on an individual's creativity. Leveraging insights from this test or others like it, schools and businesses can craft educational resources and training programs to boost these aspects and enhance an individual's creative abilities.

---

[33] See, for example, https://en.wikipedia.org/wiki/Torrance_Tests_of_Creative_Thinking; Kuo, Tsung-Hsien and Han-Kuang, Tien (2022). Enhancing the effects of creativity training for business school students through art-based methods and blended learning, *Education and Training*, 64(5), 642-661; Myszkowski, Nils et al. (2015). Managerial creative problem solving and the Big Five personality traits: Distinguishing divergent and convergent abilities, *Journal of Management Development*, 34(6). 674-684.

The Componential Theory of Creativity[34]

Teresa Amabile, the proponent of the Componential Theory of Creativity, postulates that creativity entails generating ideas or outcomes that are new and relevant to specific objectives pursued by the individual. She articulates that creativity emerges from four interrelated factors, three of which originate within the individual, and one stems from the external surroundings. These elements are encapsulated as follows:

- **Domain-relevant skills**: Refers to the individual's personal abilities, proficiency, and understanding concerning the task or issue being addressed, encompassing areas like digital transformation, leadership, and business models, among others.

- **Creativity-relevant skills**: This encompasses personality traits such as the individual's mindset, cognitive processes, vision, and strategic approaches that promote the cultivation and utilization of creativity.

- **Task motivation**: Represents the level of enthusiasm, fulfillment, and pleasure derived from achieving the set objectives.

- **The external situation**: Denotes the societal and physical contexts in which the individual operates, acting either as a facilitator or hindrance towards realizing desired outcomes, including aspects like the organization's tolerance for risk-taking, accessibility to necessary resources, and government support of entrepreneurship.

In brief, Teresa Amabile's theory proposes that creativity emerges from the interplay of several factors. These include individual skills, strategic thinking, motivation, and the surrounding environment. The theory emphasizes the collaborative nature of these aspects. It highlights that

---

[34] Amabile, Teresa M. (2012). Componential Theory of Creativity, *Harvard Business School*, Working Paper 12-096. https://www.hbs.edu/ris/Publication%20Files/12-096.pdf; Xu, Xiao-Jun and Chen, Xiao-Ping (2017). Unlocking Expatriates' Job Creativity: The Role of Cultural Learning, and Metacognitive and Motivational Cultural Intelligence, *Management and Organization Review*, 13(4), 767-794; Men, Chenghao et al. (2022). How abusive supervision climate affects team creativity: the contingent role of task interdependence, *European Journal of Innovation Management*, 25(4), 1183-1199.

inherent traits like ability do not solely determine creativity but are also significantly influenced by external factors. Undoubtedly, this theory holds value for both personal growth and various sectors of the economy, including education, entrepreneurship, and corporations.

Sternberg's Investment Theory of Creativity[35]

In 1991, Robert J. Sternberg and Todd I. Lubart published an article entitled 'An Investment Theory of Creativity and Its Development.' They proposed that creativity can be understood through the lens of decision-making, akin to investing in the stock market. Wise investors purchase shares at low prices, which others avoid due to pessimism, and then sell these shares at higher prices once others regain interest. Similarly, creativity involves investing time and effort into novel ideas, seeking new opportunities, and overcoming challenges to achieve optimal outcomes.

The authors identified six resources essential for creativity:

- Intellectual Processes: These encompass an individual's cognitive abilities, including redefining and solving problems effectively.

- Knowledge: Refers to an individual's understanding and familiarity with a particular area of interest, such as business strategy.

- Intellectual Style: This describes how an individual approaches critical thinking and processes information.

- Personality: This encompasses an individual's personal characteristics, including risk tolerance.

- Motivation: This is the individual's drive and commitment to engage in creative endeavors.

---

[35] Sternberg, Robert J. and Lubart, Todd I. (1991). An Investment Theory of Creativity and Its Development, *Human Development*, 34(1), 1-13; Beine, Jeff (2007). Evaluating Sternberg's investment theory of creativity: Are innovators widely-distributed throughout the professions and what do they have in common? Kent State University ProQuest Dissertation & Theses, 3313801.

- Environmental Context: This includes the support and encouragement an individual receives from others and external factors.

The Social Network Theory of Creativity[36]

Social Network Theory posits that creativity isn't born in a vacuum; it flourishes through an individual's social network and interactions. This network's collective value, social capital, encompasses a wealth of resources an individual can tap into, including ideas, information, moral support, and financial access. Factors like one's position within the network, the strength of connections, and the diversity of engaged networks all play crucial roles.

The theory emphasizes that creativity isn't solely a product of individual effort and hard work. It also hinges on connections and interactions with others who serve as valuable sources of inspiration. Creativity is a social phenomenon nurtured within a social context. The theory distinguishes between strong and weak ties. Strong ties, like those with family and close friends, provide essential support but might limit exposure to new and diverse ideas. Conversely, weak ties, such as colleagues and acquaintances, offer access to fresh perspectives, information, and other resources that can fuel the creative process.

The Four C Model of Creativity

In 2009, Kaufman and Beghetto introduced the 4Cs model of creativity, categorizing creativity into four distinct types[37]:

- Little-c: This refers to everyday creativity, which is prevalent among most individuals.
- Big-C: This denotes eminent creativity, typically associated with notable individuals.

---

[36] See, for example, Granovetter, M. S. (1973). The Strength of Weak Ties. American Journal of Sociology, 78(6), 1360-1380; Cote, Robert (2019). The Evolution of Social Network Theory: Perceived Impact on Developing Networking Relationships, American Journal of Management, 19(3). 19-34; Perr-Smith, Jill Elaine (2002). The social side of creativity: *An Examination of a social network perspective*, Georgia Institute of Technology Pro Quest Dissertation & Theses, 3031439.

[37] Kaufman, James C. and Beghetto, Ronald A. (2009). Beyond Big and Little: The Four C Model of Creativity, *Review of General Psychology*, 13(1), 1-12.

- Mini-c: This type encompasses creativity inherent within the learning process.

- Pro-c: This represents developmental or professional-level creativity.

The authors highlighted that prior research had primarily focused on two forms of creativity—Big-C and Little-c. They aimed to broaden the understanding of creativity by introducing new categories and expanding the scope of the creativity process. The Big-C category includes renowned historical figures and influential personalities such as Winston Churchill, Charles Darwin, Albert Einstein, and Steve Jobs. Little-c creativity, or everyday creativity, involves domain-specific skills like technical expertise, specialized talents, self-discipline, and willingness to take risks. Mini-c creativity includes personal insights and interpretations, highlighting the creative potential within learners. Conversely, Pro-c creativity pertains to accomplished individuals in the creative field, exemplified by figures like Mark Twain and Pablo Picasso.

The Four Ps of Creativity[38]

The preceding discussions in this chapter illustrate how scholars have approached the topic of creativity from various angles. Among these explorations, the Four Ps Creativity Theory offers another perspective. This theory suggests that creativity encompasses four primary aspects: Person, Process, Press, and Product, as outlined below:

- **Person**: This dimension focuses on the individual's personality traits, behaviors, and motivations, including skills, willingness to explore new experiences, curiosity, and adaptability in thinking.

- **Process** pertains to individuals' methods or strategies to generate innovative ideas or solve problems.

---

[38] Runco, Mark A. (2018). The Four Ps of Creativity: Person, Product, Process, and Press, Research Gate, https://www.researchgate.net/publication/325981320_The_Four_Ps_of_Creativity_Person_Product_Process_and_Press; Jordanous, Anna (2016). Four PPPerspectives on Computational creativity in theory and in practice, *Connection Science*, 28(2), www.tandfonline.com; Chislett, David (2018). The Four Ps of Productivity, https://davidchislett.com/the-4-ps-of-creativity.

- **Press**: This aspect considers the environmental conditions that foster or obstruct creativity. Elements such as peer influence or pressure, organizational encouragement, and availability of crucial resources fall under this category.

- **Product**: The culmination of the creativity dimensions, the product could, for example, range from an idea, a book, or artwork.

The theory posits that these four dimensions of creativity are interconnected, suggesting that the individual, their environment, and the resulting output interact. Like other theories of creativity, the Four Ps model serves as a guide for educators, organizational leaders, and policymakers at the government level. It helps them understand the essence and elements of creativity, enabling them to meet the prerequisites necessary for fostering creativity effectively.

Summary

Graham Wallas's "The Art of Thought" (1926) established a foundational framework for understanding the creative process, dividing it into four stages: preparation, incubation, illumination, and verification. This model has significantly influenced modern perspectives on creativity, underscoring the necessity of a systematic approach to generating innovative ideas. Educators and professionals have adopted the framework to develop assessments, such as the Torrance Tests of Creative Thinking, which aim to evaluate creativity across various domains. These assessments focus on measuring fluency, flexibility, originality, and elaboration, thereby acknowledging the complexity of creativity, which is shaped by internal capabilities and external environments.

Teresa Amabile's Componential Theory of Creativity builds upon this foundation by identifying creativity as a multifaceted construct influenced by domain-relevant skills, creativity-relevant skills, task motivation, and the external situation. This theory emphasizes the role of individual attributes, motivation, and contextual factors in the creative process, advocating for a comprehensive approach to fostering creativity. Similarly, Robert J. Sternberg and Todd I. Lubart's Investment Theory conceptualizes creativity as an investment, highlighting the importance of intellectual processes, knowledge, intellectual style, personality, motivation, and environmental context in the creative endeavor. Both theories underscore the need for a holistic view of creativity, considering the interplay between individual skills, motivation, and the broader environment.

The Social Network Theory of Creativity introduces the notion that creativity is a social construct reliant on an individual's social network for resources and inspiration. This theory differentiates between strong and weak ties, recognizing that both are integral to creativity. Strong ties offer emotional support, while weak ties provide access to new ideas and resources, illustrating the importance of social interactions in the creative process. Kaufman and Beghetto's Four Cs model of creativity further expands our understanding by categorizing creativity into little-c (everyday creativity), big-C (eminent creativity), mini-c (creativity in learning), and pro-c (professional-level creativity), thus broadening the definition of creativity to encompass a wide range of activities and achievements.

Finally, the Four Ps Creativity Theory provides a comprehensive framework for understanding creativity, encapsulating the Person (individual traits and motivations), Process (ideation methods), Press (environmental influences), and Product (creative output). This model integrates the individual, their environment, and the creative outcome, offering a holistic perspective on creativity. Each theory contributes to a nuanced understanding of creativity, highlighting the intricate balance between individual attributes, environmental influences, and creative output.

Questions

1. What are the four stages of the creative process outlined in Graham Wallas's model?
2. Besides individual skills, what other factors does Teresa Amabile's Componential Theory of Creativity consider important for the creative process?

3. The Social Network Theory of Creativity suggests that strong and weak ties within an individual's social network are valuable for creativity. What is the reason for this?

4. Kaufman and Beghetto's Four Cs model differentiates between various types of creativity. Can you name one category and give an example?

Appendix 5
SELF-TEST QUESTIONNAIRE

The Four Ps Theory of Creativity

Question 1: Which of the following is NOT one of the Four Ps in the Creativity Theory?

    A) Product
    B) Process
    C) Place
    D) People

Question 2: What does the "Product" aspect of the Four Ps Creativity Theory refer to?

    A) The physical goods produced
    B) The service offered
    C) Physical goods, services, ideas, etc.
    D) None of the above

Question 3: In the Four Ps Creativity Theory context, what does "Process" imply?

    A) The steps taken to produce a product or deliver a service
    B) The methods used to market a product
    C) The techniques employed to innovate
    D) All of the above

The Creative Entrepreneur

Question 4: Which of the following is NOT a component of the "People" aspect in the Four Ps Creativity Theory?

    A) Employees

    B) Customers

    C) Investors

    D) Suppliers

Question 5: How does the "Perspective" aspect contribute to the Four Ps Creativity Theory?

    A) By offering a fresh viewpoint on existing problems
    B) By focusing solely on financial outcomes
    C) By emphasizing traditional methods over innovative ones
    D) By ignoring external factors

Question 6: In the Four Ps Creativity Theory, what is the primary goal of optimizing the "Process"?

    A) To reduce costs
    B) To increase efficiency
    C) To enhance customer satisfaction
    D) All of the above

Question 7: Which of the following is NOT a strategy under the "People" aspect of the Four Ps Creativity Theory?

    A) Fostering a culture of innovation
    B) Prioritizing employee training
    C) Ignoring feedback from customers
    D) Encouraging collaboration among teams

Question 8: What does the "Perspective" aspect suggest about approaching creativity?

    A) It emphasizes sticking to established norms
    B) It advocates for a broad range of viewpoints
    C) It focuses solely on technological advancements
    D) It ignores societal trends

Question 9: In the context of the Four Ps Creativity Theory, why is it important to consider the "Product" aspect?

    A) Because it directly impacts profitability
    B) Because it influences consumer behavior
    C) Because it determines the success of the business
    D) All of the above

Question 10: Which of the following statements accurately describes the role of "Process" in the Four Ps Creativity Theory?

    A) It is irrelevant to the overall success of a project
    B) It helps in streamlining operations
    C) It has no impact on innovation
    D) It is only concerned with cost reduction

Question 11: According to the Four Ps Creativity Theory, how should "People" be involved in the creative process?

    A) Only at the beginning stages
    B) Throughout the entire process
    C) At the end of the project
    D) Only during brainstorming sessions

Question 12: What does the "Perspective" aspect encourage in the Four Ps Creativity Theory?

    A) Narrow-mindedness
    B) Tunnel vision
    C) Open-mindedness and curiosity
    D) Ignorance towards external influences

Question 13: What is the significance of considering "Process" in the Four Ps Creativity Theory?

    A) It ensures consistency in output
    B) It guarantees uniformity in execution
    C) It leads to innovation
    D) It prevents deviation from plans

Question 14: Which of the following is NOT a benefit of incorporating the "People" aspect into the Four Ps Creativity Theory?

    A) Enhanced team morale
    B) Improved communication within the organization
    C) Increased resistance to change
    D) Broader perspective on problem-solving

Question 15: According to the Four Ps Creativity Theory, how does the "Perspective" aspect influence creativity?[39]

    A) By limiting the scope of ideas
    B) By encouraging the exploration of new possibilities
    C) By focusing on immediate gains
    D) By ignoring long-term implications

---

[39] Correct answers are: 1(C), 2(C), 3(A), 4(C), 5(A), 6(D), 7(C), 8(B), 9(D), 10(B), 11(B), 12(C), 13(C), 14(C), 15(B).

Chapter 7
DESIGN THINKING FOR CREATIVITY AND INNOVATION

> "I don't think outside of the box;
> I think of what I can do with the box."
>
> Erin Patterson

Chapter Objectives

- To learn about both soft and hard skills.

- To understand the target audience by gaining deep insight into user needs through research.

- To improve problem-solving by enhancing creative and innovative problem-solving skills.

- To boost creativity by cultivating adaptability and encouraging out-of-the-box thinking.

Creative skills[40] are essential for high performance and achievement in all areas of life, from entrepreneurship and the arts to science and other human endeavors. People are not born with fixed skills readily applicable in the real world. Skills are developed and honed through

---

[40] See, for example, Weichselbraun, Albert et al. (2024). Anticipating Job Market Demands—A Deep Learning Approach to Determining the Future Readiness of Professional Skills, *Future Internet*, 16(5), 144; Kapur, Radhika (2024). PROFESSIONAL SKILLS: VITAL IN LEADING TO ENHANCEMENT OF CAREER PROSPECTS AND LIVING CONDITIONS OF THE INDIVIDUALS, *International Journal of Information, Business and Management*, 16(3), 117-126.

continuous learning and education throughout one's life and career. The choice of skills to pursue and cultivate depends on several factors, including an individual's career path, their eagerness and capacity to learn, and the availability of an external support system.

Moreover, the rapid expansion of artificial intelligence (AI), particularly generative AI, has led to the emergence of innovative products and services. This advancement, coupled with the increasing complexity of new challenges and the heightened global competition faced by businesses, necessitates acquiring soft and hard skills among entrepreneurs, executives, educators, policymakers, and the broader societal landscape. Regardless of these factors, the faster one learns, the sooner desired outcomes can be achieved. Acquiring skills requires strategic planning, dedication, and perseverance.

Skills Categories

Problem-solving is a major challenge for human beings, whether the issue involves finding food, securing a job, seeking economic opportunities, achieving excellence, or fostering creativity. Regardless of the problem, sharp skills are often necessary to overcome obstacles and challenges. Authors classify these skills into two main categories: soft skills and hard skills[41], as discussed below:

Soft Skills

To foster creativity, innovation, and success, individuals must possess unique attributes that empower them to attain their objectives. A fundamental necessity is the mastery of soft skills, particularly essential in design thinking, which emphasizes human-centric problem-solving. This array of social and cognitive abilities covers several dimensions:

- Communicating clearly and intelligently, free from ambiguity, with others.

---

[41] See, for example, Podolchak, Nazar et al. (2024). Modern world: methods of soft and hard skills development for the managers to be successful, *Administratie si Management Public*, 42, 145-157; Fantozzi, Italo C. et al. (2024). Soft Skills, Attitudes, and Personality Traits: How Does the Human Factor Matter? A Systematic Review and Taxonomy Proposal through ProKnow-C Methodology, *Businesses*, 4(2),156.

- Listening attentively to others with respect and without interruption.
- Avoiding confrontations and knowing how to resolve conflicts effectively.
- Approaching challenges with an understanding and empathetic mindset.
- Appreciating cultural diversity and promoting inclusivity.
- Learning about various leadership styles and effective team management techniques.
- Upholding organizational and professional ethics.
- Acting responsibly and considering the broader implications of one's actions.
- Developing strategic thinking and a clear vision for the future.

Hard Skills

Hard or technical skills are a set of learnable and teachable capabilities that can be applied in an individual's chosen field. These skills have become increasingly important in complementing soft (human) skills[42], particularly in areas like design thinking. Their influence extends into fields traditionally seen as immune to such skills as human resources management, literature, and law. Hard skills, which are deployable across various economic sectors and industries, are highly critical and valuable. Here are some examples:

- Financial management: knowledge of basic accounting and financial principles, financial analysis, and budgeting.
- Technology proficiency: Using software programs to analyze and interpret data and make informed decisions. This is a growing field of analytics.

---

[42] To explore the difference between hard and soft skills, see, for example, Birt, Jamie (2024). Hard Skills vs. Soft Skills: What's the Difference, www. indeed.com.

- Managerial fundamentals, including project management, strategic planning, and critical resource management.
- Foreign language familiarity, including Spanish and French.
- Cybersecurity: Skills and technology to protect organizations from external threats and thefts.
- Graphic design, including creating presentations, social media posts, and other visual objects.
- Digital marketing, including content marketing and digital transformation.
- Cloud computing. Basic familiarity with platforms like Google Cloud and Azure is essential for many entrepreneurial ventures and organizations.

The Customer

A society's consumers (or users) encompass all entities, including individuals, families, groups, organizations, and government agencies. For many business firms, such as Microsoft and McDonald's, consumers are typically dispersed worldwide. These customers vary in life stages, income levels, and economic status. Additionally, they differ in taste, lifestyle, education, culture, and beliefs. The common denominators among customers are the desire to consume or acquire goods and services of better quality at a reasonable price, with a preference for convenience and speedy delivery.

Clearly, the strength or weakness of consumer demand for goods and services affects employment, investment, and the national economy. Conversely, a drastic decline or increase in demand for a business's offerings will substantially impact its profitability and potentially its growth and survival. Intelligent providers, including entrepreneurs, recognize the importance of investigating consumer desires for goods and services and their willingness to pay to satisfy them. Market analysis and design thinking[43] are effective approaches to meet users' demands.

What's Design Thinking?

Design thinking is a systematic methodology for innovative problem-solving, regardless of the problem's complexity. It emphasizes collaboration, flexibility, and continuous improvement. By taking a logical approach, it aims to understand users' needs and discover alternative solutions and the best ways to meet them efficiently. With the advent of AI and generative AI as augmenting tools, design thinking is gaining increasing acceptance within the business community and other organizations.

Design Thinking: The stages

Design thinking consists of several stages, as discussed below:

1. Learn about the intended user's needs, aspirations, and expectations for and experience with the product. Use available data, interviews, questionnaires, and other practical methods to gain the desired knowledge about the user's needs. Create a visual map of the user's feelings and perception. This stage is normally referred to as empathize.

2. Having collected the necessary information and the target user, define the problem to be addressed. A problem is defined as the

---

[43] See, for example, Matthee, Machdel and Turpin, Marita (2019). Teaching Critical Thinking, Problem-Solving, and Design Thinking: Preparing IS Students for the Future, *Journal of Information Systems Education*, 30(4), 242-252; Menon, Bethy B. et al. (2023). Developing an entrepreneurship model using the design thinking approach and emotional intelligence for sustainable wellness among the young generation, *Cogent Business & Management*, 10(3); Vendraminelli, Luca et al. (2023). Design thinking: a strategy for digital transformation, *Journal of Business Strategy*, 44(4). 200-210. Ericson, Jonathan D. (2022). Mapping the Relationship Between Critical Thinking and Design Thinking, *Journal of the Knowledge Economy, 13(1), 406-429*; Kummitha, Roma K. R. (2018). Institutionalizing design thinking in social entrepreneurship: A contextual analysis into social and organizational processes, *Social Enterprise Journal*,14(1), 92-107; Petersen, Julia (2021). Design Thinking and Interdisciplinary Collaboration: Using The 5 Principles of Design Thinking to Increase Student Engagement in Disciplines Outside their Major, *Michigan Academician*, 48(1), 68.

difference between the current state of affairs and the desired state of affairs.

3. Upon formulating the problem statement, develop 3-to-4 creative goals to address the problem and specific steps (objectives) for each goal to address the problem. A creative statement of the problem and its potential solutions should be derived from the free flow of ideas of the participants or team members. A common technique utilized in this regard is brainstorming. This stage is called ideate, which envisions ways and means to address the problem at hand.

4. The next stage is to create a visual representation (a prototype or model) of the intended end result of the design thinking. The prototype can take different forms, such as a sketch on paper or interactive software, which will help the team or the investigator to study and identify various scenarios about the product's functioning.

5. Finally, prototype testing to ensure its viability and performance. The test can be done with or without the user's presence, and often, the end product requires certain modifications or changes.

Design Thinking vs. Traditional Problem-Solving Approach

Both design thinking and the traditional approach to problem-solving share some commonalities but exhibit significant differences. At their core, these methodologies seek to address issues through human intervention and necessitate the allocation of resources. They are utilized by individuals and organizations alike to achieve desired outcomes. However, their applications diverge in several key aspects:

- User-centric focus: Unlike traditional problem-solving techniques, design thinking emphasizes gathering insights from users' feedback, needs, aspirations, and emotional states. This approach is inherently interactive and adaptable, allowing for a more nuanced understanding of the problem at hand.

- Time and cost implications: Design thinking tends to be more time-intensive and expensive than conventional methods. This is due to the necessity of iterating through prototype cycles and incorporating expertise from various disciplines to tackle problems effectively.

- Promotion of learning and innovation: Design thinking fosters a culture of learning, continuous improvement, experimentation, and innovation within problem-solving contexts. In contrast, traditional problem-solving often relies on analytical and logical reasoning, adopting a more linear approach to issue resolution.

- Complexity suitability: Design thinking is particularly effective for addressing complex, ambiguous challenges and those requiring innovative solutions. Conversely, the traditional method is better suited for problems that are clearly defined and straightforward.

This comparison highlights each approach's unique strengths and limitations, suggesting that the choice between them should be based on the nature of the problem being addressed and the project's specific goals.

Design Thinking and Entrepreneurship[44]

Entrepreneurship involves introducing innovative goods and services that fulfill customer needs and wants. This process entails conducting market research and analysis to assess competitive dynamics, market size, and target clientele and devising effective business strategies to capture consumer demand and secure success. Conversely, design thinking represents a customer-centric, comprehensive, and adaptable approach well-suited for application within entrepreneurial ventures. It empowers entrepreneurs to comprehend their target audience's requirements and ambitions, enabling them to deliver suitable products. Furthermore, design thinking can facilitate the entrepreneur's efforts in product

---

[44] See, for example, Elzo, Alves A. et al. (2021). Entrepreneurship, Business Model and Design Thinking in Brazilian Small Enterprise, *Barranquilla*, 19 (3); Patel, Samir and Mehta, Khanjan (2017). Systems, Design, and Entrepreneurial Thinking: Comparative Frameworks, *Systemic Practice and Action Research*, 30(5), 515-533.

research and development, leading to the creation of innovative, sought-after products. Additionally, it can aid in formulating marketing and other strategic plans necessary for overcoming challenges in both domestic and international markets.

Summary

This chapter emphasizes the importance of creative skills in achieving high performance across various domains, including entrepreneurship, arts, science, and more. It argues that skills are not innate but developed through continuous learning and education. Personal interests, career paths, and the availability of support systems influence the choice of skills to cultivate. The rise of AI, especially generative AI, has highlighted the need for soft and hard skills across different sectors, underscoring the importance of lifelong learning and skill acquisition for adaptability and success.

Soft skills, crucial for fostering creativity and innovation, include communication, empathy, conflict resolution, and strategic thinking. These skills are essential for effective design thinking and a human-centered problem-solving approach. On the other hand, hard skills, which are teachable and applicable in many fields, range from financial management and technology proficiency to cybersecurity and graphic design. These skills are becoming increasingly relevant across various sectors, highlighting the value of technical competencies alongside interpersonal skills.

The chapter also discusses the significance of understanding consumer needs and preferences, emphasizing the role of market analysis and design thinking in meeting these demands. Design thinking, characterized by empathy, ideation, prototyping, and testing, offers a systematic approach to solving complex problems. It contrasts with traditional problem-solving methods by focusing on user needs and facilitating innovation and learning.

Lastly, the chapter discusses entrepreneurship, noting its reliance on innovative products and services that cater to customer needs. It suggests that design thinking, emphasizing understanding customer requirements, particularly benefits entrepreneurs, aiding in product development and strategy formulation. This approach enables entrepreneurs to navigate challenges in both local and international markets, underscoring the relevance of design thinking in entrepreneurial ventures.

Questions

1. What are the two main categories of skills discussed in this chapter?
2. What is the main purpose of design thinking?
3. How does design thinking differ from the traditional approach to problem-solving?
4. How can design thinking benefit entrepreneurs?

Chapter 8
DESIGN THINKING TECHNIQUES

> "You learn techniques to understand principles. When you understand the principles, you will create your own techniques."
>
> Alain Gehin

Chapter Objectives

- To explore the main techniques in design thinking.
- To learn about the role of empathizing in design thinking.
- To study the persona creation technique.
- To become familiar with the Six Thinking Hats method.

Like other applied business fields such as management and marketing, entrepreneurship relies on a toolbox of techniques and analytical methods, including statistical analysis, to aid entrepreneurs and decision-makers. These techniques, ranging from simple to complex, act as investigative and analytical tools to address organizational problems. However, effective deployment requires consideration of the decision-maker's judgment, experience, and resource availability. When used thoughtfully, these problem-solving techniques offer several benefits:

- Comprehensive analysis: They ensure all relevant factors are considered for a viable solution.

- Enhanced decision-making: They guide the selection of the most effective decision.

- Improved quality: They elevate the overall quality of the decision-making process.

- Reduced risk: They help avoid impulsive decisions with potentially catastrophic consequences.

As outlined in the preceding chapter, design thinking is a methodology focused on understanding human needs, aspirations, preferences, and emotions. Typically, it is divided into five interactive stages: (a) empathizing, (b) defining, (c) ideating, (d) prototyping, and (e) testing. Each stage employs specific techniques and serves unique purposes, as detailed below:

Empathizing

The primary objective of this phase is to gather comprehensive insights into the target individual's feelings, perceptions, attitudes, desires, concerns, and related sentiments regarding a particular product, service, item, or issue. This is achieved through interviews, questionnaires, or other relevant tools. A common technique employed during this stage is the creation of an empathy map, which is structured into four quadrants:

- Says: This quadrant captures the target individual's spoken expressions concerning the interview topic, including inquiries about a product's features.

- Thanks: Here, the individual's thoughts on the subject matter are summarized, focusing on aspects like the product's utility.

- Does: This quadrant records the individual's observable behaviors, such as searching for the product online.

- Feels: This quadrant encapsulates the individual's emotional reactions to the product, highlighting potential benefits of purchasing.

Below is an example of an empathy map for an individual planning to apply for a Master's in Business Administration (MBA) degree.

Says:

- Expresses confusion about program requirements.
- Ask for guidance on selecting the right specialization.
- Voices concerned about meeting admission criteria.

Thinks:

- Wonders if the program aligns with career goals.
- Considers the financial investment required.
- Doubts their eligibility due to academic performance.

Does:

- Researches program specifics and admission requirements.
- Consult with academic advisors or mentors.
- Prepares application materials, including essays and transcripts.

Feels:

- Excited about the opportunity to further their education.
- Overwhelmed by the application process.
- Nervous about potential rejection.

An empathy map

Says:	Thinks:
• Expresses confusion about program requirements. • Asks for guidance on selecting the right specialization. • Voices concerned about meeting admission criteria.	• Wonders if the program aligns with career goals. • Considers the financial investment required. • Doubts their eligibility due to academic performance.
Does:	Feels:
• Researches program specifics and admission requirements. • Consult with academic advisors or mentors. • Prepares application materials, including essays and transcripts	• Excited about the opportunity to further their education. • Overwhelmed by the application process. • Nervous about potential rejection.

This empathy map and subsequent analysis can help the university admission office visualize a potential MBA applicant's thoughts, feelings, perceptions, and concerns, offering insights for designing solutions and addressing critical issues to improve their application experience.

As mentioned, empathy maps are effective tools for organizations to collect firsthand insights into user experiences. The maps applications span various domains, such as traditional and digital marketing campaigns, product development, customer service, and numerous other sectors within and outside business operations.

Persona Creation[45]

The design thinking methodology has expanded in recent years to include various techniques and approaches for generating detailed descriptions of target users' behavior, feelings, demographics, and other attributes as they interact with products, services, systems, and more. Persona creation, as a logically structured methodology, involves the following steps:

1. Problem definition: Identify the fictional target audience (personas), their attributes, and the subject matter of interest (e.g., a product).

2. Data collection and research analysis: Gather necessary data about the fictional users' goals, desires, habits, and more. Data sources include published research, observations, online surveys, or face-to-face interviews. Analyze the collected data to learn about users' behavior patterns, needs, and trends, creating typical personas that resemble actual users.

3. Team deliberation: Discuss the created personas among team members, designers, or other stakeholders to ensure a user-centered design.

4. Refining: Refine, improve, and validate the created personas to guide the design. The objective is to ensure the user persona accurately reflects the intended user type.

What Kind of Data to Collect?

In user-centered analysis, gathering detailed data is essential to arrive at the most accurate depiction of the intended target audience. The data

---

[45] See, for example, Jansen, Bernard L. et al. (2022). How to Create Personas: Three Persona Creation Methodologies with Implications for Practical Employment, *Pacific Asua Journal of the Association for Information Systems*, 14(3). 1; Fergnani, Alessandro (2019). The future persona: a futures method to let your scenarios come to life, *Journal of Future Studies, Strategic Thinking, and Policy* 21(4), 455-466. Salminen, Joni et al. (2024). Persona preparedness: a survey instrument for measuring the organizational readiness for deploying personas, *Information Technology and management*, 25(2), 173-198;

includes the following:

- Age range of the target users
- Geographic location (e.g., state, region)
- Occupation
- Consumption patterns
- Skills and hobbies
- Personal goals
- Income
- Shopping habits
- Challenges and pain points
- Unmet needs and desires
- Usability and design preferences
- Career aspirations
- Preferred communication channels
- Level of formal education
- Interests.
- Lifestyle.

The data produced can be organized into categories to facilitate the depiction of persona creation, as demonstrated in the example provided:

Persona Profile: Jada Abrahams

Demographic Information:

- Age: 29
- Gender: Female
- Location: Baltimore, Maryland

- Education level: Holds a Bachelor's degree in Business
- Occupation: Works in Accounting

Overview: Jada Abrahams is a committed professional with over six years of experience in a medium-sized business organization. She aims to further her business studies, focusing on strategic management. Given her family obligations and professional duties, she wants to pursue an online degree program at a university.

Educational Goals:

- To deepen her understanding and skills in business strategy.
- To harmonize her career and family roles efficiently.
- To achieve a master's degree within the forthcoming two years.

Challenges Encountered:

- Balancing limited free time between work and family commitments.
- Difficulty in locating flexible and affordable educational opportunities.
- Struggling with some course materials' complexity and theory-heavy nature, preferring more applied learning approaches.

Pain and pleasure Points:

- Frustration with the slow progress and numerous prerequisites of conventional academic programs.
- Challenges in applying theoretical concepts to her professional role.
- Overwhelmed by the multitude of graduate online programs and lack of clear guidance on selection.
- Prefers acquiring knowledge through educational apps and online resources.

Learning Preferences:

- Prefers structured lectures, video content, and real-world application exercises, favoring asynchronous learning formats.
- Engages more actively through interactive assessments and project-based learning.
- Values collaborative discussions and teamwork in learning activities.

Technology Proficiency:

- Utilizes computers, smartphones, and tablets for professional and personal purposes.
- Employs social media platforms for networking and communication.

Visual Representation: The persona of Jada Abrahams serves as a model for individuals seeking advanced business education through online platforms without compromising their lifestyle. This profile encapsulates her ambitions, objectives, and preferences, guiding the development of an online learning environment tailored to the needs of learners akin to Jada Abrahams.

The Six Thinking Hats[46]

The Six Thinking Hats is an innovative approach to managing organizational meetings, introduced by Edward de Bono. de Bono believes the main challenge in thinking is confusion, as people often try to consider too many aspects simultaneously—emotions, information, hopes, creativity, and more. This method allows a group to address organizational problems in formal meetings by focusing on one type of thinking at a time. The aim is to organize discussions and make meetings more meaningful and productive.

de Bono recommends dividing the overall thinking in meetings into six hats: white, yellow, red, black, green, and blue. Each hat represents a different mode of thinking, ensuring orderly, focused, and productive

---

[46] de Bono, Edward (1985). Six Thinking Hats, Boston, Little Brown, and Company.

discussions. Organizations face various problems, some caused by external factors, such as the economy, and others by internal factors, such as employee issues.

Typically, organizations create committees to address these problems and develop recommended solutions. However, many committees are ineffective at problem-solving due to a lack of understanding of committee management protocols. The Six Thinking Hats approach outlines a protocol for managing committees. A problem is often viewed as the gap between the current and desired affairs. In many organizations, the key goal of committee meetings is to recommend solutions to eliminate or minimize the impact of problems, such as:

- Resource scarcity.
- Customer service and acquisition.
- Scope of operations/activities.
- Technology adoption.
- Competitive advantage.
- Survival and growth.
- Conflict resolution.
- Strategic initiatives.

de Bono classifies problems into three types:

1. Problems that require more information for their solution.
2. Creative restructuring involves problems that require no new information but a rearrangement of existing information.
3. Problems of no problem indicate that the organization needs to realize an issue.

The Hats Thinking Concepts:

The White Hat

White Hat thinking deals with facts and figures about the problem, issue, or situation under discussion. It does not consider opinions or interpretations and is a neutral mode of thinking. For example, the chair might ask committee members to provide their white hat thinking about the economy, requesting only the facts.

The Red Hat

The Red Hat deals with intuition, hunches, and personal impressions—attributes related to emotions and feelings. It focuses on the non-rational aspect of thinking. Wearing the red hat allows individuals to express their feelings about a problem, such as saying, "The hell with it; that's how I feel about the issue."

The Black Hat

Black Hat thinking is about a negative assessment of the situation but in a logical manner. It highlights what is wrong, the risks, dangers, and errors, focusing on critical thinking. For instance, a committee member might say, "In our past experience, lowering prices hasn't worked; let's find another solution."

The Yellow Hat

The Yellow Hat represents positive and optimistic thinking, focusing on the benefits of a solution and how to make things happen. Under the yellow hat, suggestions are made to improve something.

The Green Hat

Green Hat thinking involves new ideas, concepts, alternatives, and approaches. It is concerned with creativity and strategic thinking. For example, a committee member might suggest outsourcing the company's marketing activities.

The Blue Hat

The Blue Hat is the control hat; it organizes the committee's thinking and determines which other hats to use and when. It defines the subjects towards which the thinking will be directed. For instance, a committee chair might suggest that participants investigate the issue further and develop alternative solutions.

In conclusion, the Six Thinking Hats approach aims to make formal meetings more productive by helping participants focus on different aspects of problems logically, sequentially, and controlled.

Summary

Entrepreneurship relies on various techniques and analytical methods, including statistical analysis, to help decision-makers. These techniques, which range from simple to complex, serve as tools to address organizational problems and improve decision-making. Effective use requires consideration of the decision-maker's judgment, experience, and resources. Benefits include comprehensive analysis, enhanced decision-making, improved quality, and reduced risk.

Design thinking, a methodology for understanding human needs, typically involves five stages: empathizing, defining, ideating, prototyping, and testing. Empathizing gathers insights into individuals' feelings and behaviors using tools like empathy maps, which are divided into quadrants: says, thinks, does, and feels. This helps visualize user experiences and improve solutions.

Persona creation involves defining a fictional target audience, collecting data, analyzing behavior patterns, and refining personas to ensure accurate user representation. Data includes demographics, goals, challenges, and preferences, helping create detailed user profiles.

The Six Thinking Hats, introduced by Edward de Bono, is a method for organizing discussions in meetings by focusing on one type of thinking at a time. The hats represent different thinking modes: White (facts), Red (emotions), Black (negative assessment), Yellow (positive thinking), Green (creativity), and Blue (control). This approach aims to make meetings more productive by addressing problems logically and sequentially.

Questions

1. What are the five stages of the design thinking methodology?

2. How do empathy maps help in understanding user experiences?

3. What is the purpose of persona creation in user-centered analysis?

4. How does the Six Thinking Hats approach improve the productivity of meetings?

Chapter 9
Positive Reinforcement and Entrepreneurial Success Factors

"Keep your face always toward the sunshine – and shadows will fall behind you."

Walt Whitman

Many individuals are driven by emotions and pride in their endeavors or planned activities. Consequently, they are highly sensitive to direct or indirect feedback regarding their actions or intentions. Positive reinforcement is crucial in supporting these individuals, especially when their efforts align with desirable outcomes for themselves, their organizations, and society. Fledgling entrepreneurs, in particular, are risk-takers who take the initiative to establish new ventures and deserve societal encouragement, blessing, and support for their boldness and courage to create new jobs and offer innovative goods and services.

Chapter Objectives

- Understand the impact of positive feedback.
- Appreciate the power of encouraging words.
- Familiarize yourself with inspiring quotes.
- Learn how to inspire others.

Positive Reinforcement

Positive reinforcement, an applied concept to real-world situations, has increasingly gained the attention of executives, labor experts, authors, and others in recent years as an effective approach to motivating employees to exert extra efforts to increase output and improve the quality of goods and services. In this chapter, we propose to utilize positive reinforcement to encourage and incentivize fledgling entrepreneurs to grow and expand their business ventures for their benefit and that of society. So, what is the positive reinforcement?

The concept is defined as "a response to someone's behavior that is intended to make that person more likely to behave that way again." (Merriam-Webster Dictionary). It's "an increase in the probability of occurrence of some activity because that activity results in the presentation of a stimulus or of some circumstances." (American Psychological Association). Moreover, Lonczak (2019) suggests that positive reinforcement can be understood as follows: Rewarding behavior is more likely to be repeated. The author lists more than 30 examples of workplace positive reinforcement[47].

Experts have approached positive reinforcement from different perspectives. For example, Hubbart (2024), in referring to published research, Hubbart reiterates the importance of positive reinforcement by pointing out that positive reinforcement in an organizational setting enhances morale increases productivity and augments the retention level, while negative reinforcement is detrimental to employees' morale and commitment. Kapur (2023) asserted that positive reinforcement is a path that leads to personality development.

Knippen et al. (1997) emphasized that the right timing must accompany appropriate positive reinforcement. Petrova (2017) found that positive reinforcement influences students' motivation for learning and education. Jennings (2024) subscribes to the belief that humans are hard-wired for empathy and compassion. Moreover, Lanivich et al. (2021) believe that entrepreneurs' characteristics affect entrepreneurial outcomes through interaction with their environment and the

---
[47] Lonczak, Heather S. (2019). Positive Reinforcement in the Workplace, www.postivepsycholgy.com.

characteristics, in turn, are relevant predictors of early entrepreneurial outcomes.

Examples of Positive Reinforcement in Organizations[48]:

Scholars and others have discussed a variety of positive reinforcement examples that have been utilized particularly in mid-sized and large organizations, including the following:

- Skill development programs (For example, technical skill draining).
- Employee ambassadors' program (For example, providing funds for travel and conference attendance to represent the company).
- Wellness initiatives (for example, healthy snack options in the office).
- Recognition programs (For example, annual awards ceremonies).
- Flexible workspaces (For example, quiet rooms in the office).
- Mentorship opportunities (For example, cross-functional training).
- Community involvement (For example, matching funds for charitable contributions).
- Personalized career pathways (For example, company consultation service for employees' career advancement)
- Celebratory events (For example, welcoming parties for new hires).

---

[48] Sources: helpfulprofessor.com > positive-reinforcement-examples 21 Positive Reinforcement Examples that Work! (2024).
www.employeeconnect.com > effective-strategies-positive-reinforcement-workplace. Effective Strategies for Positive Reinforcement at Workplace. www.connectncareaba.com > blog > positive-reinforcement. How Positive Reinforcement Works: Examples Included. www.eliassen.com > blog > elas-blog-posts > positive-reinforcement-in-the-workplace Positive Reinforcement in the Workplace - Eliassen Group. www.quora.com > What-are-some-examples-of-positive-reinforcement-in-learning
What are some examples of positive reinforcement in learning?

- Autonomy in decision-making (For example, employees' input in process priority).

- Verbal Praise (For example, Edward, I really appreciate your dedication and commitment to our organization).

- Public Recognition (For example, company-wide recognition of employees' achievement).

- Monetary Bonuses (For example, offer a monetary bonus at Christmas).

- Financial incentives (For example, offer stock options).

- Flexible work arrangements (For example, offer flexible start/end times).

- Professional development (For example, offering a subsidy for college courses).

- Extra time off (For example, extra vacation days).

- Team celebrations (For example, team happy hours in fancy hotels).

- Personalized gifts (For example, customized watches).

- Autonomy and responsibility (For example, a promotion to a higher decision-making level).

- Work-life balance initiatives (For example, on-site babysitting facility).

Entrepreneurial Success Factors

Authors employ various terms such as success factors, critical success factors, or key success factors to denote elements or activities essential for ensuring the success of a business enterprise (Wikipedia). These factors are also the essential business components necessary for optimal performance and success (Indeed)[49]. In the context of entrepreneurial ventures, these factors constitute the fundamental activities entrepreneurs

---

[49] Indeed https://www.indeed.com/career-advice/career-development/what-are-success-factors

must undertake to sustain and grow their ventures. The activities include the following:

- Crafting a viable business strategy for the venture. This involves the development of the vision for the venture, creating key goals, and conducting market and financial analysis.
- Building a competent organization involves acquiring talents, adopting appropriate technology, and instituting the venture's core values.
- A focus on innovation, quality output, and excellent customer service.
- Building strategic alliances with suppliers, investors, and others.

Scholars have extensively discussed the key success factors that influence entrepreneurial success in the marketplace. For instance, Mai and Van (2023)[50] pointed out that empirical analysis unveils that (a) ecosystem factors, (b) organizational learning, and (c) creativity are the factors that significantly influence entrepreneurial success. In a literature survey, Aryadita et al. (2023)[51] concluded that researchers consider the key to success factors for fledgling entrepreneurs' startup ventures to include (a) the entrepreneur's knowledge, (b) experience, (c) competence, (d) characteristics, and (e) founding team. Lanivich et al (2021)[52] suggest that nascent entrepreneurs who participate in pre-venture assistance programs are more likely to achieve success in their endeavors. In a study about social entrepreneurship, Rwehumbiza and Hyun (2024)[53] revealed that social entrepreneurs are motivated (a) by

---

[50] Mai, Khuong, N. and Van Thanh N. (2023). Entrepreneurial Ecosystem Affects Organisational Learning, Creativity, and Success, *Cogent Business & Management*, 10(1).

[51] Aryadita, Himawat et al. (2023). Founders and the success of start-ups: An integrative review, *Cogent Business & Management*, 10(3).

[52] Lanivich, Stephen E. et al. (2021). Nascent Entrepreneur Characteristic Predictors of Early-stage Entrepreneurship Outcomes, *Journal of Small Business and Enterprise Development*, 28(7), 1095-1116.

[53] Rwehumbiza, Kalangari and Hyun, Euniung (2024). Unlocking the Factors That Motivate Social Entrepreneurs to Engage in Social Entrepreneurship Projects in Tanzania: A Qualitative Case Study, *Administrative Science*, 14(2), 31.

their individual needs, (b) goals, and (c) the satisfaction they derive from witnessing the positive impact of their work on others.

The Road to Success

Highly successful individuals, wealth experts, and others offer sound advice to young people, including fledgling entrepreneurs. They encourage these individuals to practice self-generated positive reinforcement. For instance, Warren Buffett, a renowned investor, believes that success in life hinges on 12 key decisions[54]. He suggests the following personal choices:

- The decision to nurture curiosity.
- The decision to get started.
- The decision to find mentors.
- The decision to be bold.
- The decision to be healthy.
- The decision to nurture relationships.
- The decision to plan for afterward.
- The decision to cut your losses.
- The decision to laugh.
- The decision to teach.
- The decision to do nothing.
- The decision to give back.

Summary

Positive reinforcement motivates individuals, particularly fledgling entrepreneurs, to excel in their endeavors. These individuals are highly sensitive to feedback and thrive on positive reinforcement that supports

---

[54] Warren Buffett Says True Success in Life Comes Down to Just 12 Key Decisions. Here's Your Checklist, Inc. August 18, 2024.

their efforts and encourages them to continue pursuing their goals. By recognizing the importance of positive reinforcement, organizations can enhance employee morale, productivity, and retention levels. Executives, labor experts, and authors have increasingly recognized the effectiveness of positive reinforcement in motivating employees to produce better outputs and improve product/service quality.

Positive reinforcement is defined as a response to someone's behavior that makes them more likely to repeat that action. It increases the likelihood of an activity occurring due to the presentation of a stimulus or certain circumstances. Experts have explored positive reinforcement from various angles, highlighting its benefits in organizational settings, educational contexts, and personal development. Examples of positive reinforcement in organizations include skill development and wellness initiatives, recognition programs, mentorship opportunities, and community involvement.

Key success factors for entrepreneurial ventures include crafting a viable business strategy, building a competent organization, focusing on innovation and quality, and establishing strategic alliances. Scholars have identified several factors influencing entrepreneurial success, such as ecosystem conditions, organizational learning, and creativity. Successful individuals like Warren Buffett emphasize the importance of self-generated positive reinforcement, suggesting that fostering curiosity, finding mentors, being bold, and nurturing relationships are crucial for achieving success. Organizations can foster a supportive environment encouraging growth and innovation among fledgling entrepreneurs by implementing these strategies and leveraging positive reinforcement techniques.

Questions

1. What is positive reinforcement, and how does it work in the workplace?
2. Can you provide examples of positive reinforcement techniques used in organizations?

3. How can leaders effectively implement positive reinforcement to motivate employees?

4. What are some benefits of using positive reinforcement in the workplace, and how does it impact employee performance and retention?

Chapter 10
ARTIFICIAL INTELLIGENCE (AI): THE ENTREPRENEUR'S WEAPON

"Artificial intelligence is not a substitute for human intelligence; it is a tool to amplify human creativity and ingenuity."

Fei-Fei Li

Jensen Huang, the CEO of NVIDIA Corporation, once stated that "AI will be the most transformative technology of the 21st century. It will impact every industry and aspect of our lives." This assertion supports the notion that the entrepreneurial landscape for opportunity acquisition is rapidly evolving due to the deployment of advanced artificial intelligence (AI) technologies, including chatbots, customer service and retention tools, recruitment platforms, and talent acquisition software. As a result, the transformative potential of AI should attract fledgling and other entrepreneurs who seek to harness cutting-edge technology to drive growth and sustainability for their business ventures[55]. Indeed, AI, considered the revolutionary technology of this century, is swiftly creating new opportunities for businesses worldwide.

---

[55] A comprehensive literature review found that AI is becoming an important component of entrepreneurship activities {Siddiqui, Daniya et al (2024). Artificial Intelligence in Entrepreneurship: A Bibliometric Analysis of the Literature, *Journal of Global Entrepreneurship Research*, 14(1), 13}. The implications of the profound positive impact of AI technology on entrepreneurship are suggested to involve four areas of the business enterprise: (a) opportunity generation, (b) decision-making processes, (c) performance enhancement, and (d) organizational education and research. {Giuggioli, Guglielmo and Massimiliano, Matteo P (2023). Artificial Intelligence as an Enabler for Entrepreneurs: A Systematic Literature Review and an Agenda for Future Research}.

Chapter Objectives

- To enhance understanding of AI.
- To familiarize oneself with AI technologies.
- To grasp the importance of AI for entrepreneurial ventures.
- To understand the guidelines for selecting appropriate AI technology.

AI and Entrepreneurs[56]

Entrepreneurs should develop a strategic vision recognizing AI technology's potential to expand business operations from local to national and eventually international markets[57]. This approach will support more informed decision-making and boost efficiency across human and key organizational resources. It's widely acknowledged that AI presents numerous opportunities for new entrepreneurial ventures and small businesses to increase effectiveness, efficiency, productivity, and competitiveness. AI innovative technologies can enable startups and small businesses to compete with larger corporations by leveraging advanced analytics, automation, and predictive capabilities.

Entrepreneurial ventures are designed to thrive and expand rather than stagnate or disappear. The growth of these ventures is intrinsically linked to business success. Therefore, how does one measure the success of an entrepreneurial venture? Success can be evaluated from various perspectives, such as:

The introduction of new or improved products and services through innovation.

- Improved operational efficiency.

---

[56] Regarding the application of new technology, it is asserted that ChatGPT adoption in entrepreneurship endeavors significantly and positively affects entrepreneurs' attitudes toward digital entrepreneurship. {Doung, Cong D (2024). ChatGPT Adoption and Digital Entrepreneurial Intentions: An Empirical Research Based on the Theory of Planned Behaviour, *Entrepreneurial Business Economics Review*, 12(2), 129-142}.

[57] It's suggested that the entrepreneurs' strategic mindset greatly influences the success of AI startups. {Lee, Byunguk et al. (2024). Enhancing the Competitiveness of AI Technology-Based Startups in the Digital Era, *Administrative Sciences* 14(1), 6}.

- Expansion of market share and increased sales.
- Growth in revenue and profitability.
- Adoption of winning competitive strategies.
- Visionary leadership.

What's AI?

Standard University's Human-Centered Artificial Intelligence program[58] emphasizes that artificial intelligence was first introduced in 1955 by John McCarthy, who characterized it as "the science and engineering of creating intelligent machines." Our current efforts are directed towards developing systems that can learn and adapt, mirroring human capabilities and transcending the limitations of pre-programmed behaviors.

Conversely, IBM[59] indicates that AI encompasses many technologies to enhance machine intelligence. IBM further notes that AI represents the transformative technology of our era, serving as a versatile tool that can be applied to both individual tasks and comprehensive processes. Distinguishing it from conventional software, generative AI has the potential to supplement human intellect and facilitate unprecedented advancements in business productivity. Regardless of how one defines AI, it is broadly accepted as the driving force behind investments, leading to economic advancement and prosperity for nations that harness this revolutionary and rapidly expanding technology.

What is AI Technology?

Ten types of artificial intelligence technologies[60] are the focus of research, learning, and teaching, particularly within higher education institutions. These technologies are also widely applied across various industries in the United States and other developed nations. They are:

---

[58] https://hai.stanford.edu/sites/default/files/2023-03/AI-Key-Terms-Glossary-Definition.pdf
[59] https://www.ibm.com/artificial-intelligence
[60] M, Pavitra (2024). AI Techniques: Mastering Machine Learning, Deep Learning, and NLP, www.https://clickup.com.

- Machine learning (ML)
- Supervised and unsupervised learning (S&UL).
- Deep learning (DL).
- Natural language processing (NLP).
- Text preprocessing (TP).
- Part-of-speech (POS) tagging.
- Named entry recognition (NER).
- Sentiment analysis (SA).
- Computer vision (CV).
- Automation and Robotics (A&R).

The benefits of AI technology include the following[61]:

- AI solutions enable entrepreneurs to streamline operations.
- They assist in developing strategic initiatives and decision-making.
- They help improve customer relationships and retention.
- They allow the business to gain critical insights into customers' needs and behavior.
- They lower costs by reducing labor-intensive tasks and improve productivity as well.
- They assist in talent identification, recruitment, promotion, and retention.

---

[61] The AI technology applications are many and growing. For example, in the tourism and hospitality industry, the following are reported to have been utilized: (a) chatbots, (b) augmented reality, (c) drones, (d) kiosks/self-service screens, (e) QR codes, (f) booking systems, (g) robots, (f) virtual reality, (g) machine translation, (h) voice assistance. {Sousa, Alan E et al. (2024). The Use of Artificial Intelligence Systems in Tourism and Hospitality: The Tourists' Perspective, *Administrative Sciences*, 14(8), 165}.

The Creative Entrepreneur

- They support efforts toward leadership development and team cohesiveness.

- AI solutions create the venture's sustainable competitive advantage, which is crucial for the business's survival and growth.

A Closer Look at the Technology[62]

Automation has rapidly expanded across various economic sectors in recent years, driven by the pursuit of efficiency and cost-effectiveness. This technological revolution encompasses various applications, including automatic drones, autonomous vehicles, automated cybersecurity systems, enterprise resource planning, hiring processes, robotics, human-machine interfaces, and smart home devices. Entrepreneurs would be wise to explore these and other automation systems as potential avenues for their business ventures.

Data analytics represents a rapidly expanding area of statistical application across various sectors, including business and the public sector. Data analytics is crucial in boosting profitability and refining operational efficiency and decision-making processes in business. This application often employs spreadsheets, data mining software, and data visualization techniques. Given its ability to handle vast datasets, data analytics offers numerous benefits to businesses, particularly in the following domains:

- Gaining insights into customer spending patterns, preferences, and market dynamics.

- Identifying market and industry trends, along with understanding the competitive environment.

- Implementing measures to mitigate or prevent market risks.

---

[62] See, for example, Hardik Shah, (2024). Advantages of Artificial Intelligence (AI) for Your Business; King, Kylie et al, Impact of Artificial Intelligence (AI) on Entrepreneurship, Penn State Social Research Institute, https://evidence2impact.psu.edu/resources/impact-of-artificial-intelligence-ai-on-entrepreneurship/ Elliott, Jessica, AI Tools That Can Help You Start, Run, and Grow Your Small Business, https://www.uschamber.com/co/run/technology/how-ai-benefits-businesses; Investopedia (2024). Data Analytics: What It Is, How It's Used, and 4 Basic Techniques, https://www.investopedia.com/terms/d/data-analytics.asp; Dataforest (2024). Data Analytics: The Future of Business, https://dataforest.ai/blog/the-importance-of-data-analytics-in-todays-business-world

- Assessing potential financial risks across various market conditions is often accomplished through predictive analytics, which employs AI algorithms.

Companies like IBM, Oracle, SAP, Tableau Software, Google, and Microsoft have developed various AI-related technologies tailored for businesses and other organizations. These tools encompass:

- Personalized recommendation systems for advertising, e-commerce, and content streaming.

- Resource management software for effective project management and resource allocation.

- Business strategy software for comprehensive planning and performance management.

- Financial analysis software for financial planning, data analysis, reporting, and investment decision-making.

- Marketing analysis software for content management, customer segmentation, sentiment analysis, customer personalization, sales forecasting, and campaign performance evaluation. Healthcare software is designed for disease diagnosis, customized treatment plans, and patient outcome prediction.

- Educational software aimed at personalizing learning experiences, adapting teaching methodologies, and evaluating student performance.

- Retail and e-commerce software intended to improve online shopping experiences via personalized recommendations and effective inventory management.

Deployment of AI Technology

The deployment of AI technology is a significant challenge for entrepreneurial ventures, especially those in their early stages. Determining which AI technologies or techniques to adopt and the associated costs is a crucial dilemma. This is often compounded by entrepreneurs' limited understanding of available options and their specific needs. The following guidelines aim to address this issue[63]:

- Understand your industry, target market, and economic sector within the context of the North American Industry Classification System (NAICS) classification (Chapter 8).

- Analyze your business's strengths, weaknesses, opportunities, and threats (SWOT analysis) to determine its future direction.

- Gain knowledge about the types of technology utilized in your industry.

- Evaluate the technology, talent, and training requirements, considering financial constraints, and set specific, achievable goals.

- Learn about various AI technologies and their functions to identify those that align strategically with your business vision and operations.

- Ensure the security and safety of your technological assets.

- Periodically assess the benefits and limitations of the technology and anticipate future needs as your business grows and expands.

Benefits of AI Deployment

AI offers substantial and enduring advantages to both entrepreneurs and the broader business sector. It excels at processing and condensing vast datasets to identify economic trends, market shifts, consumer income levels, attitudes, spending habits, environmental changes, and other pivotal socioeconomic factors, thereby aiding in effectively managing entrepreneurial ventures. Here is an overview of these benefits:

---

[63] See, for example, Willhard, Doug (2024). Conventional Business Models Weren't Cutting It — See How Innovating With AI is Changing the Game for Startups, *Entrepreneur*, https://www.entrepreneur.com/science-technology/4-strategies-for-harnessing-new-technologies-as-a-growing/470357; Dominic Chalmers et al (2021). Artificial Intelligence and Entrepreneurship: Implications for Venture Creation in the Fourth Industrial Revolution, *Entrepreneurship Theory and Practice* 45(5) 1028-1053; Siu, Eric, Choosing the Right AI Solution for Your Business, https://www.singlegrain.com/blog/a/ai-solution-for-your-business/

- Cost Reduction, Enhanced Efficiency, and Productivity Boosts: Automating routine tasks like accounting, customer service inquiries, and operational planning leads to cost savings, increased efficiency, and higher productivity.

- Resource Optimization: AI facilitates the optimal utilization of essential resources, including sales teams, raw materials, and other inputs, ensuring they are used effectively and efficiently.

- Risk Management: By analyzing and predicting financial and market trends, AI helps mitigate risks associated with business operations.

- Innovation in Products/Services: Utilizing advanced AI tools like Open AI, GPT Plus, and Gemini can drive innovation in products and services, keeping businesses ahead of the competition.

- Strengthened Customer Relationships: Analyzing customer data and implementing personalized strategies significantly improves customer relationships and loyalty.

- Superior Decision-Making and Strategic Planning: Specialized software powered by AI enhances decision-making processes and enables more effective strategic planning.

- Advanced Financial Practices: Tasks such as budgeting, expense monitoring, and portfolio management become more streamlined and accurate through AI integration.

- Competitive Advantage: Achieving a competitive edge becomes easier with AI's assistance in adopting a more analytical approach to employee management, customer service, and resource allocation.

Summary

Entrepreneurial ventures are designed to grow and succeed, with their expansion closely tied to business success. Success in entrepreneurial ventures can be measured through various metrics such as introducing new or improved products/services, enhancing operational efficiency, expanding market share and sales, increasing revenue and profitability, adopting successful competitive strategies, and demonstrating visionary leadership. These indicators reflect the health and progress of a venture, highlighting areas of strength and opportunities for improvement.

Artificial Intelligence (AI), first introduced by John McCarthy in 1955, has evolved into a transformative technology that mirrors human intelligence and adapts to changing environments. AI technologies, including machine learning, deep learning, natural language processing, and computer vision, are being researched, taught, and applied across various industries. These technologies enhance individual tasks and contribute to comprehensive processes, offering a versatile toolset for businesses looking to innovate and improve.

Automation and data analytics represent significant technological advancements that have permeated multiple sectors, aiming for efficiency and informed decision-making. Automation covers various applications, from drones and autonomous vehicles to cybersecurity systems and smart home devices, providing entrepreneurs with innovative solutions to streamline operations and reduce costs. On the other hand, data analytics leverages AI to analyze vast datasets, offering insights into customer behavior, market trends, and financial risks, which are crucial for strategic planning and risk mitigation.

Deploying AI technology poses challenges for early-stage entrepreneurial ventures due to the need to understand the technology's applicability, costs, and alignment with business goals. However, AI offers substantial benefits, including cost reduction, enhanced efficiency, resource optimization, risk management, product/service innovation, strengthened customer relationships, superior decision-making, advanced financial practices, and a competitive advantage. These benefits underscore the importance of integrating AI into business operations to stay competitive and achieve long-term success.

Questions

1. What key metrics are used to gauge an entrepreneurial venture's success?

2. How do AI technologies, such as machine learning and natural language processing, contribute to the growth and success of businesses?

3. Can you explain the role of automation and data analytics in improving entrepreneurs' operational efficiency and decision-making processes?

4. What are the benefits of deploying AI technology in entrepreneurial ventures, and how can they contribute to achieving a competitive advantage?

Chapter 11
MANAGING YOUR OWN COMPANY

"I never lose. Either I win or learn."

Nelson Mandela

Chapter Objectives

- To enhance understanding of management principles.
- To develop skills in managing teams and other resources.
- To gain insight into essential organizational structure and strategy.
- To evaluate company performance.

Picture this: You've finally assembled your team, secured the funding, and harnessed the latest technology. Your startup is ready to take flight. But as you stand at the threshold of launching your venture, you realize that success depends on more than clever ideas and cutting-edge tools. What foundational management principles will guide your company toward sustainable growth? This chapter delves into the essential managerial insights every aspiring entrepreneur needs to know. It's not just about having a great product or service—it's about building a sustainable business enterprise, fostering a positive company culture, and making strategic decisions that drive success.

What is Management?

The concept of "management" has been viewed from various perspectives by authors over the years[64]:

1. Management refers to a group of top executives responsible for overseeing an organization.

2. Management encompasses the act of accomplishing tasks and objectives.

3. Management consists of managerial functions that include organizing, controlling, coordinating, and guiding workflows and employees to achieve the organization's vision and key goals.

4. Management serves as the organizational engine for decision-making processes.

5. Management is an academic discipline incorporating teaching, learning, research, and degree-granting activities.

These diverse perspectives highlight the multifaceted nature of management[65], demonstrating its importance in various contexts within organizations and academia.

What are the Managerial Functions?

Managers' essential functions, particularly in mid-sized and large organizations, revolve around marketing, operations, accounting/finance, and human resources. Each of these areas operates according to its specialized nature. These functions include planning, monitoring, organizing, and executing plans.

---

[64] The following are two definitions of management: (1) "Management involves coordinating and overseeing the work activities of others so their activities are completed efficiently and effectively". Robbins, Stephen P. and Coulter, Mary (2014). *Management*, Upper Saddle River: New Jersey, Pearson Education, Inc; p. 7, (2) Management is "The planning, organizing, leading, and controlling of human and other resources to achieve organizational goals efficiently and effectively" Jones, Gareth R. and George, Jennifer M. (2014). *Contemporary Management*, New York: NY, McGraw-Hill/Irwin, Inc. p.5.

[65] Certo, Samuel, C. and Certo, S. T (2014). *Modern Management*, Upper Saddle River: New Jersey, Pearson Education, Inc, p.5.

On the other hand, the role of the chief executive officer in these companies extends beyond day-to-day management. It centers around setting the company's vision, strategy (the roadmap), and key goals (desired targets). The CEO oversees overall activities and conducts meetings with key stakeholders such as customers and vendors.

The functions of an entrepreneur running a startup company are similar to those of a mid-sized enterprise manager and chief executive officer combined, though on a smaller scale. This includes crafting vision, goals, strategies, and the responsibility of planning, organizing, monitoring, and leadership. In brief,

- Managers' core responsibilities vary based on company size and their position in the organizational structure.
- CEO roles go beyond operational management.
- Startup entrepreneurs face similar challenges as larger company managers, but on a smaller scale

Management Principles

Management is a multifaceted field encompassing theory, practice, and discipline. Its universal scope and profound impact make it crucial for entrepreneurial ventures and other organizations to be managed effectively to achieve their missions, visions, and strategic objectives.

Management principles are guiding frameworks that promote orderly workplace dynamics, efficient resource allocation, and logical distribution of authority and decision-making within an enterprise. These interconnected principles collectively form essential rules for successful managerial practices within organizations.

Various management principles are derived from diverse sources, including military strategies, economic theories, sociological studies, and psychological insights. Others have emerged through empirical research and successful managerial experiences.

Several fundamental management principles widely applied in well-managed enterprises include:

1. Chain of Command (Scalar Chain): This principle establishes a hierarchical governance structure where lower-level managers directly report to higher-level managers, extending throughout the organization. Violating this principle can lead to workplace chaos due to confusion about decision-making authority. For example, the practice of micromanagement in some companies violates this principle.

2. Span of Control: This principle recommends limiting the number of subordinates reporting to a manager or supervisor. The rationale is that managers have limited physical and mental capacity daily. Excessive subordinates may result in decreased efficiency and potentially poor decision-making. Factors influencing the optimal span of control include job nature, employee skills, organizational size, economic sector, and manager experience.

3. Unity of Command: According to this principle, one leader should oversee employees performing similar organizational functions. Multiple leaders managing the same group can cause instability due to conflicting instructions.

4. Authority and Responsibility Parity: This principle states that employees should receive commensurate authority with delegated responsibilities, regardless of position.

5. Division of Labor: This widely applied economic principle involves dividing organizational functions (e.g., marketing, accounting) into appropriate units, departments, and divisions. Departmentalization increases productivity and output by specializing in various aspects of the organization.

Company Structure and Strategy

Organizations, regardless of their nature, must choose their organizational structure. The shape and complexity of this structure depend on factors such as the organization's size, operations, and target market. Generally, larger organizations have more complex structures.

For example, Toyota's organizational structure has more managerial levels than Foot Locker.

There are several forms of organizational structure, including:

1. Functional Structure: This is the most widely utilized design in business. It groups tasks by business functions such as marketing, logistics, research & development, and human resources.

2. Divisional Structure: This structure is suitable for large organizations. Functional activities can be performed within divisions. The structure can be designed based on products, processes, geographical areas, or customers.

3. Matrix Structure: This is the most complex of all designs. It utilizes both vertical and horizontal flows of authority and communication.

Entrepreneurial startup companies typically have a flat structure with one management layer (e.g., CEO and general manager). As business operations expand, additional layers become necessary to meet market demand for goods or services effectively.

A company's business strategy significantly influences its organizational structure. For instance, if a strategy dictates direct investment in several countries, the structure would be altered to accommodate global expansion.

The business strategy serves as a roadmap for the organization, created based on market analysis to ensure sufficient, sustainable demand for the company's offerings. A popular strategy for entrepreneurial companies is differentiation, which positions the offering as uniquely innovative relative to competitors. Uniqueness can take various forms, including convenience, ease of use, price, shape, speed of delivery, size, and color.

Business firms have adopted numerous strategies over the years, such as:

1. Diversification: Expanding offerings to include related or unrelated products/services

2. Integration strategy: Expanding operations through acquisitions, such as acquiring a rival company

Regardless of the major strategic initiative undertaken, companies should carefully assess the costs and benefits of the strategy.

Challenges Facing New Entrepreneurial Companies[66]

Newly established entrepreneurial ventures face numerous challenges and obstacles in achieving strategic goals and financial performance. Visionary entrepreneurs who anticipate hurdles and plan to overcome them through better decision-making and persistence may be successful in their endeavors. The main challenges include:

- The increasing desire among employees for remote work and away from office settings.
- Uncertainty in demand for goods and/or services.
- Inability to compete with larger, more resourceful companies for talent acquisition.
- Implementing policies of diversity, inclusion, and equity.
- Lack of funds and experience in emerging technologies, such as efficiently using artificial intelligence tools and applications.
- Insufficient market and industry knowledge.
- Underdeveloped business networks and lack of company recognition.

Company Performance

Company performance refers to the outcomes achieved by a company over a defined period, typically spanning one year. It measures the

---

[66] See, for example, Al-Fattal, Anas (2024). Entrepreneurial Aspirations and Challenges among Business Students: A Qualitative Study, *Administrative Sciences*, 14(5), 102; Saferdin, Wan Aisyah. B. et al. (2024). Exploring the Challenges of Engaging in Entrepreneurial Activities among Undergraduate Students: A Case Study in Malacca, *Global Business and Management Research*, 16(2s), 428-436; Sarmah, Ankita and Saikia, Bedabrat (2023). Business Challenges of the Nascent and Mature Micro Small and Medium Enterprises (MSMEs): a Comparative Analysis from India, *Journal of Global Entrepreneurship Research*, 13(1), 20.

effectiveness of management strategies, leadership, and policies. Assessing performance based on a comprehensive matrix is crucial for entrepreneurial companies that have survived in the market for two or more years. This assessment should consider several key factors, including:

1. Profitability
2. Growth in market share
3. Expansion of assets (e.g., employment, property)
4. Return on Investment (ROI)
5. Customer service and retention rates
6. Innovation (ratio of new product/service sales to total sales)

By evaluating these factors, entrepreneurs can gain valuable insights into their operational efficiency, strategic effectiveness, and overall success. This assessment helps identify areas of strength and potential improvement, guiding future business decisions and growth strategies.

A Theoretical Framework for Management[67]

As a learning, teaching, and practice discipline, does management necessitate a theoretical framework to illuminate its nature, dimensions, and functions? Much like other social sciences, such as economics and psychology, management requires a robust theoretical foundation to validate its significance and indispensability. Over the past decades, scholars have introduced many compelling theories that have significantly impacted effective organizational operations and resource allocation.

---

[67] The following articles present interesting discussions about management theories:
Miftari, Fljamur (2024). The Impact of Modern Management Theories, *UTMS Journal of Economics*, 15(1), 99-106; Thomas, Joseph (2020). Organization and Management Past to Present: Applicability to Practice in the Modern Enterprise, *International Journal of Business Strategy and Automation, 1(2), 52-61;* Kitana, Abdelkarim (2016). Overview of the Managerial Theories and Theories from the History: Classical Management Theory to Mode4n Management Theory, *Indian Journal of Management Science,* 6(1), 16-21.

The main management theories cluster around the following topics:

- The Classical School (Scientific Management).
- The Behavioral School.
- The Quantitative School.
- The Systems School.
- The Contingency School,
- The Quality Management School/
- The Learning Organization School.

Different schools of management theory emphasize various factors that influence organizational effectiveness. For instance, the Classical School focuses on aspects such as:

1. Careful worker selection and training
2. Planning, coordinating, organizing, monitoring, and evaluating tasks

The Behavioral School highlights issues like:

1. Organizational harmony
2. Conflict resolution
3. Motivating employees to increase output and improve productivity

The Quantitative School recommends applying quantitative analysis in decision-making and resource allocation. Systems Theory suggests managing the organization as a system with interconnected components, including inputs, outputs, transformation processes, and feedback loops.

The Contingency School proposes that management strategies consider the external environment's impact on the organization. The School of Quality Management emphasizes the importance of continuous improvement in organizational management.

Finally, the Learning Organization School focuses on creating, acquiring, and transferring knowledge within organizations while committing to ongoing learning and development.

Summary

Management refers to overseeing and coordinating organizational activities to achieve goals. It encompasses various functions, including planning, organizing, controlling, coordinating, and guiding employees. Management is the organizational engine for decision-making processes and is crucial for entrepreneurial ventures and large companies.

The core responsibilities of managers vary based on company size and position in the organizational structure. Chief Executive Officers (CEOs) go beyond day-to-day management by setting vision, strategy, and key goals. Startup entrepreneurs face similar challenges but on a smaller scale, handling all management aspects themselves.

Management principles provide essential rules for successful managerial practices within organizations. These include concepts like chain of command, span of control, unity of command, authority and responsibility parity, and division of labor. The choice of organizational structure depends on factors such as company size, operations, and target market. Common structures include functional, divisional, and matrix designs.

Company performance is measured over defined periods and considers factors like profitability, growth in market share, asset expansion, return on investment, customer service, and innovation. Evaluating these metrics helps identify areas of strength and potential improvement, guiding future business decisions and growth strategies. Management theories, such as those from the Classical School, Behavioral School, Quantitative School, Systems School, Contingency School, Quality Management School, and Learning Organization School, provide frameworks for understanding organizational effectiveness and developing effective management practices.

Questions

1. What are the key functions of managers in mid-sized and large organizations?

2. How do different organizational structures impact company performance?

3. What do newly established entrepreneurial ventures face some common challenges?

4. How do different schools of management theory influence organizational effectiveness?

References

Abdoulkadre, Ado and Massa, Idriss D. (2023). Creative Industries' Entrepreneurial Success: Social Capital, Networks, and Internationalization Strategy, *Journal of Comparative International Management*, 26(2), 144-158.

Aryadita, Himawat et al. (2023). Founders and the success of start-ups: An integrative review, *Cogent Business & Management*, 10(3).

Bamford, Charles E. and Bruton, Garry D. (2011). *Entrepreneurship – A Small Business Approach*, New York: NY, McGraw Hill, Inc.

Brida, Juan G. et al. (2024). How does population growth affect economic growth and vice versa? An Empirical Analysis, *Review of Economics and Political Science*, 9(3), 265-297.

Carraher, Shawn A. and Welsh, Dianne, H. B. (2015). *Global Entrepreneurship*, Dubuque: IA, Kendell Hunt, Inc.

Carter, John J. III et al. (2023). Examining the Entrepreneurial Mindset and Entrepreneurial Intentions, *Journal of Applied Business and Economics*, 25(4), 3-46.

Clapham, Maria M. and Meyer, C. K. (2924). LEADERSHIP FOR CREATIVITY AND INNOVATION, *Journal of Business and Educational Leadership*, 14(1), 49-60.

Corrales-Estrada, Maria (2020). Design thinkers' profiles and design thinking solutions, *Academia*, 33(1), 9-24.

Dasgupta, Meeta (2023). Driving Creativity and Innovation through Emotional Intelligence (EI): A Systematic Literature Review, *Journal of Innovation Management*, 11(3).

Dyantyi, Noluntu and Faleni, Nobathembu (2023). Entrepreneurship education to Stimulate Entrepreneurial Mindset in Chemistry Students, *International Journal of Research in Business and Social Science*, 12(10), 209-216.

Hisrich, Robert D. et al (2013). *Entrepreneurship*, Los Angeles, California, New York: NY, McGraw-Hill/Irwin, Inc.

Holcombe, Randall G. (2003). The Origins of Entrepreneurial Opportunities, *Review of Austrian Economics*, 16(1), 25.

Hubbart, Jason A (2024). Understanding and Mitigating Leadership Fear-Based Behaviors on Employee and Organizational Success, *Administrative Sciences*, 14(9), 225.

Jennings, Frederic B Jr (2024). The Economic Cultures of Fear and Love, *Journal of Philosophical Economics*, 17, 156-192.

Johnson, Kevin L. and Wu, Cindy (2021). Creating Entrepreneurial Opportunities as a Means to Maintain Entrepreneurial Talent in Corporations, 25(3), 327-348.

Kapur, Radhika (2023). Reinforcement of Positivity in One's Outlook is the Key in Promoting Well-being, *International of Information, Business, and Management*, 15(3), 70-79.

Knippen, Jay T. et al. (1997). Asking for positive reinforcement, *Journal of Workplace Learning*, 9(5), 163-168.

Lanivich, Stephen E. et al. (2021). Nascent Entrepreneur Characteristic Predictors of Early-stage Entrepreneurship Outcomes, *Journal of Small Business and Enterprise Development*, 28(7), 1095-1116.

Leonelli, Simona et al. (2022). Keep Dreaming: how personality traits affect the recognition and Exploitation of entrepreneurial opportunities in the agritourism industry, *British Food Journal*, 124(7), 2299-2320.

Liu, Chih-Hsing et al. (2023). Creating competitive advantage through *Management Decisions*, entrepreneurial factors, collaboration and learning, 61(7), 1888-1911.

Mai, Khuong, N. and Van Thanh N. (2023). Entrepreneurial Ecosystem Affects Organisational Learning, Creativity, and Success, *Cogent Business & Management*, 10(1).

Maran, Thomas K. et al. (2021). Motivational foundations of identifying and exploiting entrepreneurial opportunities, *International Journal of Entrepreneurial Behavior and Research*, 27(4), 1054-1081.

Neck, Heidi M. et al (2018). *Entrepreneurship,* Los Angeles: California*:* SAGE Publishing, Inc.

Petrova, Elitsa (2017). The Influence of Positive Reinforcements on Motivation for Education and Training Activities, *Journal of Economic Development, Environment, and People*, 6(3), 6-15.

Rwehumbiza, Kalangari and Hyun, Euniung (2024). Unlocking the Factors That Motivate Social Entrepreneurs to Engage in Social Entrepreneurship Projects in Tanzania: A Qualitative Case Study, *Administrative Science*, 14(2), 31.

Scarborough, Norman M. and Cornwall, Jeffrey R. (2019). *Entrepreneurship and Small Business Management*, New York, NY, Pearson Education, Inc.

Straker, David and Rawlinson, Graham (2004). *How to Invent (Almost) Anything*, Rollinsford: NH, Spiro Business Guide.

Tanner, Akan et al. (2022). Explaining U.S. Economic Growth Performance by Macroeconomic governance, 1952–2018, *Journal of Evolutionary Economics*, 32(5), 1437- 1465.

www.ingramcontent.com/pod-product-compliance
Lightning Source LLC
Chambersburg PA
CBHW052031030426
42337CB00027B/4960